WILD CARP

By Fennel Hudson:

A MEANINGFUL LIFE
A WATERSIDE YEAR
A WRITER'S YEAR
WILD CARP
FLY FISHING
TRADITIONAL ANGLING
THE QUIET FIELDS
FINE THINGS
A GARDENER'S YEAR
THE LIGHTER SIDE
FRIENDSHIP
NATURE ESCAPE
BOOK OF SECRETS
THE PURSUIT OF LIFE

Fennel's Journal

No. 4

WILD CARP

By

Fennel Hudson

2020
FENNEL'S PRIORY LIMITED

Published by Fennel's Priory Limited

www.fennelspriory.com

First shared as handwritten letters in 2009
Limited edition magazine published in 2012
eBook published in 2013
This extended edition published in 2020

Text and images copyright © Fennel Hudson 2020,
with the exceptions of images on: the Dedication
(Demus Canning), page 13 (Mike Winter), 263 and 265
(Pavol Timko), 271 (Scott Winstanley), 272 (Andy Batchelor),
273 (Les Darlington, Peter Whipp), 275 (Stuart Harris).

Fennel Hudson has asserted his right under the
Copyright, Designs and Patents Act 1988
to be identified as the author of this work.

All rights reserved. No part of this publication may be
reproduced, stored in a retrieval system or transmitted,
in any form or by any means, electronic, mechanical,
photocopying, recording or otherwise, without
the prior permission of Fennel's Priory Limited.

"Stop – Unplug – Escape – Enjoy"
and The Priory Flower logo are registered trademarks.

A CIP catalogue record for this book
is available from the British Library.

Hardback ISBN 978-1-909947-14-6
Paperback ISBN 978-1-909947-15-3
Kindle ISBN 978-1-909947-12-2
Audiobook ISBN 978-1-909947-92-4

Designed and typeset in 12pt Adobe Garamond Premier Pro.
Produced in England by Fennel's Priory Limited.

CONTENTS

Foreword 1
Introduction. 5
A Gift from the Romans? 9
Golden Dreams 15
Old Maps and Ancient Waters 21
The Moated Manor 29
A Haunted Pool 37
The Monastery Pond 43
A Trip to the Shops 49
Amongst the Secret Carp 65
Chasing Mollies 73
Double Vision 79
A Flick of the Tail. 97
On Hallowed Ground 109
A Clacking of Knobs 127
The Freeminers' Brethren 135
The Embowered 143
Beyond Midnight. 149
The Lake at the Edge of the World 155
The Sleeping Giant. 165
Steady as She Goes 183
The Monster of the Deep 189
Across the Moors 201
The Sanctuary 209
Ginger Beer and All Things Holy 217
Freedom and Forgiveness 227
The Mist of Believing. .239

CONTENTS

Return to the Folly 245
The Wild Carp of The Danube 259
The Wild Carp of Wales .267
Wild Carp Identification 281
Further Reading 285
Wild Carp Conservation 289

About the Author 291
The Fennel's Journal Series 295

DEDICATION

To the memory of Mike 'Prof' Winter,
friend, mentor and wild carp enthusiast, who
encouraged me to stick to my ideals, go in search
of my dreams, and write about my adventures.
Without him, this quest would not have been
so richly rewarding or so crucially
important to complete.

STOP – UNPLUG – ESCAPE – ENJOY

This book, and the series to which it belongs, is about freedom. It's also about the adventures to be had when pursuing one's dreams, developing and communicating one's self, and striving for a slow-paced rural life. It's your opportunity to take time out from the stresses of modern living, to stop the wheels for a while, unplug from the daily grind, escape to a quiet and peaceful place, and enjoy the simple life. Because of this, I'd like you to read it in a distraction-free and relaxing environment: your 'safe place' where you can savour quality time and, if possible, delight in the beauty of the countryside. That's why the book is pocket-sized, has a waxy cover and is printed using special waterproof ink. It's designed to be taken with you on your travels. Don't store it in pristine condition upon a bookshelf; allow it to reflect the adventures you've had. Use a leaf as a bookmark and annotate the pages with ideas of how you will honour your right to 'never do anything that offends your soul'.

The more mud-splattered, grass-stained, and pencil-scribbled this book becomes, the more you've demonstrated your ability to pursue a contented country life. So go on: live your life, be authentic, and always remember to 'Stop – Unplug – Escape – Enjoy'.

"For where your treasure is, there will your heart be also."
Matthew 6:21

FOREWORD TO THE 2020 EDITION

Wild Carp began life in 1989 when I was just fifteen years old. It's amazing to think that thirty-one years have passed since the first chapter was penned, when I was compelled to seek an old and rare strain of fish – and write about the adventure – after my physics teacher lent me the classic carp fishing books *Confessions of a Carp Fisher* by BB, and *Casting at the Sun* by Chris Yates. They had a dramatic effect on my life, setting me on a path that would lead me to many secret and wonderful pools, making new acquaintances and lifelong friends – many of whom took me under their wing and taught me how to fish traditionally and simply, for the pure pleasure of being beside water. This style of angling is captured in this book, complementing the historic and timeless quality of old carp pools, though it is fundamentally about a quest for a very special type of fish. The oldest strains of wild carp (more accurately described as *feral* carp in the UK) are so rare and at risk from predation or the hands of Man (specifically, cross breeding with modern strains of king carp introduced to old waters by anglers wishing to catch bigger fish) that this book,

History, future, and the sum of our dreams.

like the fish it describes, might become a legacy of what was, rather than what is. Thankfully, at the time of writing, I know of a handful of pools where wild carp still thrive and are cherished by those who fish for them. One day, I promise you, I will secure a pond or lake where wildies will be preserved. Until then, this book serves to remind me of some of the wonderful waters, dreams, fantasies, fish and anglers that have led me towards this yearned-for destiny. It is, without doubt, my magnum opus, if such a thing exists amongst fishing books. I take pleasure in sharing it with you, for the first time in its full extent, as it contains the principal stories from my twenty-year quest to discover the ultimate wild carp water. And whilst it ought to be a standalone

FOREWORD TO THE 2020 EDITION

book, it's included within the Fennel's Journal series in acknowledgment of my old friend and mentor Mike 'Prof' Winter. It was he who fuelled my passion for wild carp, guided my search and accompanied me on many adventures, giving me a kick up the backside to share my stories with others. If it wasn't for Mike, you wouldn't be reading this or any of the Fennel's Journal books (most of which began life as letters to him) and I wouldn't have achieved a tenth of the things I've done in my angling or writing life. Thus this book is dedicated to the memory of Mike Winter, who taught me that biggest isn't always best, that small is beautiful, that the past informs the present (and so shapes our future), and that wild carp are a living connection between people, place and time.

INTRODUCTION

Wild carp are the Holy Grail of the traditional carp angler. Whilst some anglers consider salmon to be the king of fish, or describe wild trout with elitist praise, wild carp are iconic and mythical fish that forge a living connection between past and present. Prized by the Romans, traded by Norman monks, imported by medieval landowners and worshipped by modern-day traditional anglers, wild carp are the golden-scaled and priceless bounty of those who seek the angling ideal. I am such an angler, having spent the past twenty years searching for the oldest strain of wild carp in the UK. At first, the quest was to learn about the fish; then it was to find them; finally, and with great hope and faith, it was to fish for and catch them. Eventually it became a mission for something else: to discover and preserve a seemingly 'lost' fish and a forgotten way of fishing – one that involves searching for contentment beside timeless watery places. The adventure, I'm pleased to report, is complete. I've found a pool, which I've named The Sanctuary, that is completely perfect. There are wild-like carp present. It's remote. Rugged. And very close to heaven.

You'll notice that I used the term 'wild-like' just then. This is to please the purists who would rightly point out that carp are not native to the UK and that true wild carp inhabit the River Danube, not British waters. So, to avoid confusion, when I mention wild carp in this book, I am referring to feral carp: carp that – by very definition of being transported by man – were once domesticated but which have since reverted to a feral form akin to the original wild carp. But I choose to call them wild carp, or 'wildies' for short, because 'feral' sounds too much like a once-pampered kitty that got bored drinking saucers of milk and went rummaging through dustbins. Ancient strains of carp deserve better. They're not the poor, flea-bitten and mangey relatives of a well-to-do relative; they're super fit athletes that put their overweight grandparents to shame. Time and generational reversion, in my opinion, benefit carp. Like hours on the treadmill for a doughnut-munching slob, the years away from the fish farmer's food counter serve to return these fish to a form that God, rather than Man, intended.

Twenty years. That's how long it took me to find such a fish. The adventure – as recorded in this book – began in my early teens and concluded in my mid-thirties. The first five chapters were written while I was at school. The final chapters were written recently. It's interesting to observe how my focus – and writing style – has

INTRODUCTION

evolved over these two decades. At first the writing's factual as I learn about the fish, then it's descriptive, and at the end, well, then we're into the Fennel's Priory mould of seeing things as part of the broader scheme of life. Because, for me, searching for wild carp mirrors my quest for a perfect rural life: of existing quietly in remote or forgotten places away from the stresses, turbulence and artificiality of the modern world.

If you are to search for wild carp, then you need to dream. To begin the dream, I ask that you picture a long, lean, fish; similar in shape and size to a koi carp that might swim in a garden pond, but with golden-bronze scales; its fins are a grey-brown colour, its shoulders and back are slate grey. It is living in a pond so overgrown that you can barely see the water. It's poised near the surface, basking in the afternoon sun. You stare at the fish for a while, watching its gill covers pulse in and out, its mouth open and close and its eyes twitch as it keeps watch for predators. It is moving slowly towards you.

You have just imagined a wild carp. Now, let's go and find one.

1989

I

A GIFT FROM THE ROMANS?

Imagine standing in a muddy field in mid-winter. A gale blasts from the north, crusting your clothes with ice. Your fingers are stiff, your face is numb and your back aches. It is the late nineteenth century and you are working on the largest archaeological dig that Britain has ever known, uncovering a Roman city called Silchester. There are dozens of people working alongside you, gently teasing relics from the ground. Even with all these workers, the excavation will last uninterrupted for twenty years. But you don't know this yet. What you do know is that you've just unearthed something special, a treasure hidden beneath the flooring of a room with a hearth. You've discovered a clay pot that contains the remains of a fish – a carp – which, given the age of the site, is nearly two thousand years old. It is potentially the earliest record of carp being in England. If you choose to believe…

Although 'carp' are mentioned in archaeological records such as those of Silchester, experts suggest that these fish might be other cyprinids such as roach. Although Romans are likely to have been the first to cultivate carp – Pliny the Elder wrote about carp farming in the first century – there is no mention of carp in the Domesday Book. Thus, historians studying the earliest references to carp in English literature will state that carp were introduced to the UK in the late fourteenth or early fifteenth century. Now, you can vote with your head and agree with the historians, or you can open your heart to the totally unproven and likely fictitious idea that carp were present in the UK during Roman times – even if it was as a pot of preserved food. However fantastical it may be, I hold on to the dream that the Silchester fish really was a carp and that these fish were alive in the UK in Roman times. I'm a hopeful romantic who believes in the spirit and truth of dreams, so I'm captivated by the thought that Romans might have introduced live carp to the UK as they did to other countries within their empire. And, given that I'm always seeking the cloud-like nirvana of dreamland, I hope that their descendants might still exist too, hidden in a long-forgotten pond, waiting for us to discover them.

Roman or not, the oldest strains of carp are so rare that to discover them is to connect with something so improbable as to be barely believable. To understand their journey, we need to travel back in time to 8,000 BC, when the last of the woolly rhinoceros and sabre-toothed cats walked the Earth. The history of wild carp, therefore, dates back 10,000 years when, following

A GIFT FROM THE ROMANS?

the Ice Age, they spread from the Black and Aral seas into the River Danube, eventually colonising an area of river below the Piedmont zone east of the Alps. The carp evolved in the river's strong currents, developing a streamlined head and body and a large noticeably forked tail. They also developed the ability to store large amounts of blood sugar in their muscles; enabling explosive bursts of strength but – to their captors' delight – making their flesh taste sweet.

It is believed that the Romans first reached the Danube at a location called Carnuntum (opposite modern-day Devin Castle near Bratislava, on the border between Slovakia, Austria and Hungary), conquering this area in 15BC. Carp had established in this area and were a favourite delicacy of the locals, who caught them in nets from the grassy plains when the river was in flood. The Romans, being expert fish farmers and entrepreneurial types, harvested the fish, cultivated them in ponds, and exported them to their provinces as a commercial item. (It is thought the fish were transported in wooden barrels filled with water.) The Roman roads of Europe forged westwards from Hungary through Austria, Switzerland and France. Therefore, by the time the Romans reached English shores, the carp and their domesticated descendants would have travelled an astonishing 1,800 miles.

In theory, if Roman carp were ever stocked into ponds in Britain, there is an outside chance that they could still exist today. But the probability is slim. Although some fish might have survived in very remote places, the likelihood is that once Roman rule ended (in circa 410AD) the locals would have plundered the fish stocks and eaten whatever remained. However, the Norman invasion of 1066 brought with it a resurgence of fish farming and import activity. The change in monarchy and religions at this time saw the introduction of the Cistercian order to Britain. Cistercian monks didn't have to pay taxes, so they exploited this loophole by importing and exporting vast amounts of goods. It is unproven, but carp may well have been imported from European fish farms at this time. Fortunately for us, early Cistercian monks were forbidden from eating meat during their fasting periods, so they kept stew ponds stocked with fish.

There are many Norman fishponds remaining today, identifiable by their entry in the Domesday Book. Most of them are just small shallow ponds that barely seem fit for ducks, but it is this very 'unfishable' character that conceals them from the attentions of the everyday angler. Consequently it is conceivable that if the Normans imported carp, then their strains of fish might remain. But it's not just Roman and Norman fishponds that are of interest to the wild carp hunter. Estate lakes, ponds and moats – especially if they are adjacent to country houses, manors and castles – are worthy of investigation. The reason for this is that in the fifteenth

A GIFT FROM THE ROMANS?

Image of the ideal: wildies from a Norman fish pond

century there was a trend for wealthy landowners to build ornamental ponds and lakes in their grounds as a status symbol. A gift of fish was a way of expressing wealth between these landowners, so carp imports grew to meet the demand. As the cost of maintaining country estates increased, many of these pools fell into disrepair and became overgrown as Nature reclaimed her own. The carp, in their new 'wild' surroundings, flourished. (Cultivated carp, when left undisturbed, revert through successive generations to a feral form akin to the wild carp. Nature, it seems, has a way of returning things to how they should be.)

Although feral carp can never be described as genuine wild carp, their appearance is close enough to their ancestors for them to be bestowed the title of 'wildie' or 'wild-type' by anglers. However, the giveaway sign is that all cultivated carp, even the feral descendants, have a notch at the back of their head where the shoulders start. The more cultivated the carp, or less feral, the bigger the hump of the shoulders. The true wildie of the Danube doesn't have this notch at all; the transition between its head and shoulders is perfectly smooth. The challenge for wild carp 'grail hunters' is to find a Roman, Norman or medieval pond that contains a very old strain of carp that is uncontaminated by cross breeding with modern varieties. These fish are likely to be small (wildies up to five pounds are average; a ten pound fish is a giant and a twenty pounder could be nicknamed Nessie). This is good. Fishing for wildies is the antithesis of the modern 'big carp' scene, which is all-too-serious about catching big fish. Success is not measured in pounds and ounces, rather in the age of the strain identified by the extent of feral reversion. *The older the strain, the bigger the reward.* Pursuing these fish, therefore, is to escape the noise, one-upmanship, urgency and macho chest-beating of modern angling in favour of something small, original and beautiful.

The best ponds – the ones where the oldest strains of wildies live – are the closest kept secrets in angling.

1989

II

GOLDEN DREAMS

The world of water has a way of perpetuating myths and shrouding lakes in mystery. If Loch Ness can conceal an aqueous monster, then small pools can hide a small fish. However, unlike Nessie, wild carp are real. They live in secret places, away from predation and the intrusions of modern carp varieties. In some instances, they have been undisturbed for centuries. Fishing for them would be like looking out onto a lime-lit stage, preparing to perform Hamlet, knowing that Shakespeare himself is in the audience. Your performance, dress, and the scenery around you would need to be perfect, else the connection with your audience would be lost. *Though this be madness, yet there is method in 't.* (Hamlet, Act II, Scene II.)

The concept of the perfect wildie pool is the reason why traditional carp anglers find themselves daydreaming about casting a line for these elusive fish. In our mind's eye we have crept slowly, rod in hand, to the edge of a mist-swirled pool, to see signs of these golden creatures. Bubbles rise along a nearside margin and the leaves of a water lily twitch as a fish swims past.

Your heartbeat quickens. The time is yours. You are in an undisturbed utopian state.

"Hey, Lazy!" The words rip through your dream, shattering the pool into splinters and yanking you back into reality with an undignified thump. An annoyed teacher, boss or spouse stands over you, tapping their watch and shaking their head. Your dream is gone. The carp, the anticipation, the tranquillity, are lost. You lower your head and return to the tedium of daily chores.

Eventually, after much dreaming, the dream no longer suffices. You have to physically be there, gazing at the pool and the fish, knowing that you are safe from the indignities of those who simply 'don't understand'. You vow that someday you will find the pool of your dreams and fish for this perfect strain of carp.

But where to begin the search? There are so many lakes and ponds to investigate. The proliferation of modern carp is so widespread that even if you were to identify a historic water then the chance of wildies remaining would be hopelessly slim. But the dream – the vision – burns deep inside us, keeping one's hopes alive that there must surely be an inaccessible or secret water remaining where wildies have survived. You convince yourself that they exist, awaiting your discovery. You breathe deeply, focus your thoughts, and say out loud: "The quest begins here."

Remember this moment. It will, I assure you, lead to secret, forgotten waters. Some of which can be fished; others will always remain out of reach, tormenting and inspiring you to keep hunting. It is a deeply personal journey, where each discovery enhances your appreciation for and relationship with these fish. It adds another layer of excitement to your quest.

My journey started properly this year (1989) but I've subconsciously loved the idea of 'lost' lakes and searching for treasure for years. When I was born, I inherited a library of pre- and post-war angling books. These works proved to be a revelation, describing a slow pace of life that I yearn to live. And when it comes to defining angling technique, they extol a basic approach that rejoices in art over science. It is the simple charm of man against fish that overwhelmed me, none more so than the stories of old carp caught from lost waters.

The works of Bernard Venables, Arthur Ransome, and H.T. Sheringham describe, in detail and with a sense of reverence, the character and atmosphere of traditional carp fishing.

My favourite teacher at school, Mr Hackney, learnt of my love of fishing and gave me two books: *Confessions of a Carp Fisher* by BB, and the recently-published *Casting at the Sun* by Chris Yates. They were accompanied by a note, saying, "You've found the key, now unlock the door." *Confessions* and *Casting* became my essential references. [They were later joined by *The Secret Carp*, also by Yates.] Between them, these books conjured up images of dark, brooding pools surrounded by ancient, gnarled trees, some standing, others fallen, some lying decaying in the water's edge as havens for the mightiest of fish. The crumbling walls of a long-abandoned abbey would be the only remaining sign of habitation; ivies would cascade over the stonework and across the woodland floor, signifying nature's victorious advance; and wild carp would haunt the watery depths. This vision was and is an ever-present beacon, urging me to take up the quest to find it.

The defining moment, when my obsession with wildies became irrepressible, occurred during an English lesson at school. I was standing up, reading aloud passages from Chaucer's *Canterbury Tales*, when the words on the page blurred and my language became that of Izaak Walton saying, "And my first direction

is, that if you will fish for carp, you must put on a very large measure of patience." The class looked up, my teacher double-checked her copy of the text, and I was instructed to sit down quickly before I caused further embarrassment to myself. My dreams had broken through into reality, forcing a sense of destiny upon me. I was truly obsessed with wild carp. I had to go in search of them and, in so doing, escape into the timeless depths of a long-forgotten pool.

Being fifteen and in love with an idealised image of carp will – I imagine – lead to a rather unusual adolescence. Creatures with breasts are taking second place to those with fins; nights out with friends are being cancelled in preference to time beside moonlit pools; pocket money is reserved for fishing books, bait and tackle. My priorities are established. My schoolmates will say, "Get a life", but I'll be off exploring, searching for those out-of-bounds places where wild carp swim and the best of life exists.

I've already explored many of the estate lakes, farm ponds and wooded pools close to home. Most contain tench, perch, roach and pike. A small number hold carp but, because of this, are rather too popular with local angling clubs. I've dismissed these pools and moved on, hoping to find something wilder, more forgotten and seemingly inaccessible. I have made it my mission to discover a water that is off the beaten track. Somewhere in the undergrowth of the impossible.

1990

III

OLD MAPS AND ANCIENT WATERS

Finding prospective wildie ponds is easy. All you have to do is study the oldest maps in local libraries and county records offices and look for mention of pools, fishponds and moats. The older the map, the greater the chance that a water shown might contain the strain of fish we seek. *Find the lake and find the fish.* All you then need to do is check a modern map to see if the pool still exists, then pay it a visit on a hot summer's day to see if any carp can be found basking in the sunshine.

My first visit to a library in search of wildie pools was unsuccessful. The librarian was a middle-aged woman with horn-rimmed spectacles and a face that looked like she'd spent a lifetime sucking pith from a gooseberry. My request to view her oldest and most fragile documents was met with a remark that "Children are best entertained chewing bubble gum; they have fingers sticky from today's tuck shop and yesterday's snot. Archives are no place for the youth of today. Return with a responsible adult and I will allow you to view the maps."

The following evening, after school, my mother

escorted me back to the library. The librarian was still there, walking up and down the aisles of books like an exam invigilator. I asked her if I could be allowed to look at the gardening books while my mom inspected the maps. The librarian's face softened. She put her hand on my shoulder and escorted me to the section containing books about propagation, plants and compost. As she did, she whispered to me that gardening was her deep and sometimes dirty passion and, for all her bending over in beds, she'd never had chance to 'share her love' with a young man. I smiled nervously and thanked her for her encouragement. I reached for the first book I could find: *A Beginners Guide to Plums*.

The librarian's 'guiding hand' (along the bookshelves) encouraged my belief that I would get lucky amongst the archives of older tomes and historic papers. My hopes and stamina were rewarded when, an hour later, she announced that my 'release' was imminent. Pointing to the rear of the library, she identified my mom carrying armfuls of photocopied maps. Her look of excitement indicated that many of these maps showed ponds and lakes and that I had enough information to begin searching in earnest for new waters. I also had a new friend in the librarian, who was 'literally' keen for me to learn the ins and outs of hardwood propagation.

The maps showed many lakes; some were accompanied by notations written in calligraphy, identifying evocative landmarks such as 'moat', 'fish pond' or 'quarry'. Many of these pools were off-limits. Some lay deep within keepered estates, others were adjacent to old farmhouses and one was in the garden of a country hall. But, as I would soon learn, there is a difference between 'off-limits' and those places you can visit without getting caught.

I decided to visit these pools very late in the evening or early morning when normal folk would be asleep. Fish spotting at in the half-light or dark would only be possible if a carp leapt from the water or bow-waved across the lake, but there would be less chance of me getting a thick-ear from the landowner. Carp lakes are most atmospheric in twilight, so it would be a good time to absorb the mood of a pool to determine if it had a warming or oppressive personality. An hour at dusk or dawn would be sufficient to reveal the lake's character and determine whether any wild carp were present.

Visiting at early and late hours was not as effective as I'd hoped. It aroused too many suspicions. I'd explored a handful of prospective pools but found that farmers would often be up and going about their duties at dawn and gamekeepers were out searching for poachers at dusk. At one pool, in the last hour of daylight, I was pushing my way through a thicket of brambles when I startled a nide of pheasants. The resulting ruckus attracted the attention of a gamekeeper who, before I knew what was happening, blinded me with a flashlight. I heard the terrifying 'chunk' of a shotgun closing. I threw myself to the ground as an explosion of shot peppered the foliage around me. The gamekeeper called for me to stand up. I couldn't. My heart was pounding and I was struggling to breathe. The flashlight continued to search the area but failed to see me on the woodland floor. The gamekeeper eventually lost interest and walked away, leaving me to control my emotions. I'd prepared myself for a telling-off from a displeased adult, but I wasn't prepared for a backside full of lead shot. I needed to invent a way of visiting these waters safely.

I eventually found the perfect answer: I would visit these waters on a Sunday afternoon when the countryside was busy with ramblers walking off their Sunday roasts. I would dress up as a young birdwatcher, with gaiters, walking boots, binoculars and a bright blue Pac-a-Mac cagoule. I'd take a clipboard with me, upon which would be a tick list of birds and some crude drawings of waterfowl. If a gamekeeper stopped me I would plead innocence and say that I was completing a school ornithology project. I would ask him where I could find moorhens or herons, as I needed to draw them if I were to complete my homework.

With my new foolproof strategy in place, I returned to the scene of the shotgun confrontation: The Wooded Pool. Exploring the parkland and surrounding woods in daylight was so much easier. I could see people coming from a distance, so I wouldn't have any sudden shocks to my nerves or backside.

OLD MAPS AND ANCIENT WATERS

The map in my hand was dated 1889 and showed an expansive deer park, country house and formal gardens. The lake was marked 'fish pond' and lay in the hollow of a wooded valley. Most alluringly, the lake was adjacent to the ruins of an old monastery and there was a 'Friars Oak' nearby dated 1100 AD. By looking at the scale and contours of the map I concluded that the pool was about two acres in size and fairly deep. Best of all was its location right in the centre of the estate, over four miles from the nearest road and surrounded on all sides by parkland.

Remarkably, the estate had changed little since the map was drawn. The hedgerows and wooded drives were the same and there were no new buildings. The wood that contained the lake was soon identified and I walked along a footpath until the crucial moment came, when I veered off into the 'forbidden forest'. With my clipboard in hand, I made an effort to appear lost and confused, just in case I was being watched.

The woodland appeared less impenetrable than when I visited at dusk. The brambles only grew around the perimeter of the wood and there were tracks inside for estate vehicles. Further into the wood (which was made up of oak, ash, yew and beech) the woodland floor became a carpet of bluebells and wild garlic, with the occasional clump of emerging bracken and copse of hazel. It was one of those places where mist lingers well into the day and the dawn chorus starts early.

I saw the stonework of the monastery first: sculpted sandstone that had weathered to dust in places. It had curved lintels and a gothic window, long since removed of its stained glass, which gave the building a sense of lost grandeur. Although ruined, it stood defiantly against the passing of time and a sea of nettles.

I passed the monastery and then, as the light in the wood began to brighten, saw sunlight glinting on water. My steps quickened. Soon I could see a triangular-shaped pool, fringed with reeds and overhung in places by rhododendrons. The water was murky and dark, with weed and lilies growing in it. A coot startled from the margins and a fish, probably a pike, bow-waved from the reeds as the bird pattered past.

The Wooded Pool was my first proper discovery,

idyllic in every way. I clapped my hands together and smiled. I did a little jig and then, as my excitement grew, began dancing wildly. I didn't care whether I would be allowed to fish the pool; I was just so thrilled to know that waters like this still existed. The only question was, were there any wildies present?

I never found out. My jubilations and reckless dancing had announced my presence. I heard an aggravated "Oi!" echoing towards me from within the wood. I recognised the voice as that of the keeper who had shot at me. Instead of running, I stood my ground, fumbled for my clipboard and put on my most innocent 'who, me?' face.

The keeper approached quickly, pushing aside clumps of nettles to check that I hadn't stashed any pheasants in the undergrowth. When he reached me, he raised his eyebrows and said, "Well?" I explained that I was not a poacher and was merely hoping to find some waterfowl to draw for my school project. I showed him the drawings on my clipboard and the map in my hand, pointing to our current location. Fortunately, I must have looked less like a would-be poacher and more like a boy avoiding Sunday school. The keeper's expression remained stern but not condemning. Instead, he confirmed that there were waterfowl here, but that I was on private land and should return to the footpath at the top of the hill and head home.

With a flash of inspiration, I made one last attempt to continue my quest. I said that his decision was disappointing because next term's project was on fishes and I was having difficulty finding a water containing carp. He replied sternly, "You shouldn't be asking those questions round here Sonny, I might think you were a poacher!" He tipped his hat and ushered me on my way.

As I walked back through the wood I wondered whether I would find another water as nice as The Wooded Pool. I'd come close but was now a marked child. I paused and studied the map once more. My eyes widened in horror. There, on the edge of the map, were the notes from my previous trip. They said, in bold red letters: "Lake seems promising; but beware the keeper, he's a nutter!"

1991

IV

THE MOATED MANOR

Moats are my favourite setting for catching wild carp. Their close proximity to ancient buildings, such as manor houses and castles, serves as a reminder of their long history and gives them a stately appearance.

It was during a visit to Worcestershire County Records Office that I found reference to a manor house that had served as a hiding place for soldiers during the English Civil War. I looked it up on an eighteenth century map. My eyes widened as I read the words 'moted groundes'. In the 1640s (the time of the civil war), moats could have taken many forms. Some were filled with water; others would have been little more than a boggy ditch. Even worse, they could be a stinking cesspit of sewage and kitchen waste that no marauder would dare cross. Even so, I felt compelled to follow my nose and investigate the property, wondering whether the moat contained water and, if so, if it held any carp. The following weekend saw me cycling to a village near to the manor. I asked for directions at a nearby post office and was informed that both the manor and the moat remained. Also, that the property opened to the

public each spring to display its formal gardens. By good fortune, the manor was open that day and, for a small entry fee, I could gain access to the gardens.

I returned to my bicycle and pedalled down the lanes to the manor. As I approached, I could see cars parked along its driveway and an entrance gate surrounded by dozens of people. I reached the gate, leant my bike against a fencepost, paid the entrance fee to an elderly gentleman and walked into the grounds.

The manor was an impressive building: three stories high and made of red bricks with one wing that was timber framed. Its walls were buckled as if hunched with age and its tiled roof was crinkled like a newspaper that had dried after being left out in the rain. It had stood for over three hundred years and yet looked like it could topple to the ground at any moment like a house of cards on a waiter's tray.

The moat was narrow and canal-like in front of the manor, with water lapping the bricks of the building. A double-span bridge crossed the moat at this point, allowing access to the manor. Further along, the moat separated a wildflower meadow on the nearside bank and a rose and topiary garden on the far side. To the left and right of the manor, the moat turned ninety degrees before opening out into a wider pool to the rear, its banks lined with oaks, dog rose, hawthorn and pollarded willows.

I walked towards the moat and to the hordes of

visitors who were scurrying along the garden's pathways, marvelling at the box topiary and smelling the roses in the borders. Such was their preoccupation with the Floribundas, Damasks, Gallica and Hybrid Teas that they had barely noticed the moat, even though its yellow irises and water lilies were equally as beautiful as the roses.

Standing on the bridge, I looked down into the water in search of fish. I saw a small perch lurking beneath the arches, its eyes fixed on a shoal of fry that were congregating in open water. At least the water contained fish, but did it hold any carp? I removed the rucksack from my shoulders and took a loaf of bread from inside that I had brought as 'an offering for the ducks'. I tore small pieces of crust from the loaf and threw them into the water. I then withdrew, moving into the garden to study the moat from behind the roses.

I was admiring the pale pink blooms of Rose 'Fantin Latour' when, from the corner of my eye, I noticed a swirl on the surface of the moat. I crept back to the bridge for a better look. From my vantage point I could see five dark shapes gliding slowly through the water, nudging through lily stems to get to the floating crusts. I noticed their golden-bronze scales. They were carp. But were they wildies?

I spent several hours watching the fish, concluding that they definitely looked like wildies. Then, when most of the visitors had left, I approached the man who had been collecting money. It transpired that he was the owner of the manor and his wife was the green-fingered one who had created such an idyllic garden. I mentioned my love of gardening, and also of angling, and how I had admired the manor and its moat.

The man informed me that the narrow sections of the moat were once badly silted and choked with weeds, but the more open area had always contained water and fish. It was during his restoration of the garden that the moat was dredged and water from the open area was allowed to flood through. I mentioned that I had seen carp in the moat and asked him if angling was permitted. He seemed somewhat surprised by the request, saying that there must surely be bigger ponds with larger fish available. I explained that I was an old fashioned angler seeking to fish in a peaceful and relaxing way in traditional surroundings. Other waters were too noisy, too busy, and contained fish so large that they might break my landing net.

The man smiled. I detected that he was also a quiet fellow, most at home amongst plants and meadows. Something registered between he and I, so I was granted permission to fish the moat. The only stipulation was that I could only fish after six o'clock in the evening, never at weekends, and that I must always depart before dark. I was to leave "Five of the Queen's pounds" in an envelope after each visit and, at the end of the year, provide him with a bottle of single malt.

The following evening saw me back at the Moated Manor, with fishing rod and net in hand. The carp were basking in the upper levels of the water when I arrived. I could see that they were long, lean, blunt-nosed fish with very dark bronze scales, resembling a scattering of unpolished pennies at the bottom of a wishing well. Their tails were deeply lobed, more so than a common carp's, and their fins seemed disproportionately large for their bodies.

All I could do at first was sit and watch the carp. I then tackled up my rod and net. This was to be uncomplicated, purist fishing. The minimum of tackle, the simplest of approaches and a goal to get as close to the carp as possible before casting. The bait for the evening was breadcrust, which I tore into one-inch pieces and threw into the water adjacent to the reeds. I sat back against the trunk of a willow and waited for the fish to begin feeding. Slurping noises soon betrayed the carps' appetite for bread. Three fish were working their way along the reeds. Every now and then, one of the reed stems would kick and a piece of breadcrust would disappear into a mini whirlpool.

I embedded the hook into a piece of crust and then let the bait dangle on the line before swinging it into the area of water where the carp were feeding. A fish moved to the left of my crust and then swirled beneath it. Then it drew close. As the ripples of the other fish subsided, the carp opened its lips and sucked in the bait.

THE MOATED MANOR

I quickly lifted the rod, hooking the fish. Water sprayed into the air as the fish thrashed against the line. My reel screeched and my fingers tightened around the rod. I had connected with my first wild carp.

The fish darted up and across the moat, bow waving on the surface then boring deep. In a daze, I played the fish as best I could, but I could barely track the speed at which it swam nor comprehend the stamina with which it fought. Breathless, I questioned how this fish could send me into such a trembling frenzy. The fish made a lunge down the narrow section of the moat, slicing the water with a bow wave that was followed by a stream of fizzing bubbles. I clamped down hard on the reel. The fish rose in the water then crashed violently on the surface as I pulled it back towards me and over the net. Water exploded into the air. A savage 'craaack!' echoed across the moat. The net kicked and then felt lifeless. My knees buckled and I collapsed to the ground. The line had parted. The fish was gone.

I gathered my thoughts, and then my tackle, and headed for home, not knowing that the pool I was about to fish next would be darker and more foreboding that anything I'd ever experienced.

1992

V

A HAUNTED POOL

There are some pools that woo us, as if in courtship. Others challenge, as if yearning a feisty relationship. Many exhibit the bland expression of a passing stranger. My experience at The Moated Manor proved that a carp pool could be a playful temptress, capable of building our dreams and then shattering our hopes, just as our hearts begin to flutter.

Understanding the varying moods of a lake, and knowing when to engage and when to leave, can mean the difference between a successful and a failed fishing trip. An experienced angler knows that a lake's mood can change direction as quickly as a tornado. There is no logical reason for the transformation, it just happens. One minute you can be relaxing by the side of the pool, enjoying the evening sunlight, watching bubbles appear by your float and tracking the moorhens dabbing across the pool. The next minute you feel overwhelmed, the water takes on a bleak and lifeless look, the air grows cold and it's as much as you can do to stay there a second longer. It is like looking into the eyes of a scorned lover. The Haunted Pool is such a water. As night falls, the pool adopts a hostile, almost evil, atmosphere that has the ability to strip an angler of his or her confidence, awaken their inner demons and immerse them in a waking nightmare of panic and discomfort.

The events at The Moated Manor caused me to seek an intensely atmospheric experience. I wanted to continue my quest and prove my commitment to wild carp. The Haunted Pool came to mind and so, in a moment of madness, I decided to attempt a nocturnal vigil. It was a decision I soon came to regret.

I arrived at the pool at 10pm. The day had been fine, though not warm. It was one of those dusks where the day simply rests its head in exhaustion. It had gone to bed early, awaiting a deep sleep.

The pool lay in the middle of dense woodland of oak and yew. It was shaped like the iris of an adder's eye and fringed by bracken, sallow and rowan. Previous trips had shown the water to be dark and peaty, like gazing into the brew of a well-stewed teapot. It didn't at first appear to be a particularly fertile place. The spongy, yellow, lifeless 'soil' of rotting yew leaves did little for the quality of the water. However, the pool was covered in bistort weed and supported a healthy population of carp – lean torpedoes that were deep bronze in colour, darkened by a lifetime of swimming in the shadow of a silent forest.

I decided to fish in an area where the bracken was

thinnest and the water was clear of weed. I set up my net and then my rod and reel, attaching a single swan shot to the line and tying on a size eight hook, onto which I threaded two kernels of sweetcorn. I cast the bait out into the lake and then laid the rod in a forked stick before catapulting two pouchfuls of corn around my hookbait. I knew that the ratchet of my centrepin reel would sound if a fish took line; so I lay down amongst the bracken, content to take in my surroundings.

Night fishing accentuates the atmosphere of a lake. It is as if, once darkness falls, the character of the pool announces, "I am here." I have held conversations with a lake in the past – asking how it feels and whether it will be generous and provide a fish or two during the night. Often it responds with a crashing carp, as if to say, "Yes, just wait," or a sudden gust of wind to indicate, "Maybe, let me think about it." So far, the pool had appeared quiet and forgiving. It had a relaxed feel. But I knew what it could be like and was prepared for the worst. I was potentially going to outstay my welcome. The pool would try its usual tricks – making me feel uncomfortable, edgy or impatient, bushes would rustle in the darkness and twigs would crack. I was prepared for all that. I knew that mind games contain only inner demons and that, quite possibly, the wild carp that fed during the night were bigger than anything I'd caught before. It would not be me against the fish, rather me against the lake.

Two hours passed. No fish, no activity, no ghosts. Alone in the darkness, I was away from home and suffering from fish rejection. Why me? Why now? I reeled in, put a new bait on the hook and cast out again. I retreated to the relative warmth of the bracken, to lie down and rest. The scent of the bracken, infused with the damp nocturnal air, coaxed me into a dizzy state. I had to sleep. I closed my eyes and felt the world spin into nothingness.

I was happily dreaming about hoisting aloft my first wildie when I woke with a start. My heart was pounding, my body was icy cold and I was shuddering uncontrollably. All my senses were alert, as if to warn me of imminent danger. Yet nothing moved around me. The pool looked serenely calm.

Then the sound. A terrifying, high-pitched scream followed by a gurgling groan and sudden 'thump' upon the ground. I sat, frozen, for a moment, before turning my head slowly. The sound had been close, too close. It had come from the edge of the wood. I felt compelled to investigate. I rummaged in my creel and felt what I was searching for: a lighter used to ignite my primus stove. It was empty of fuel but the flint still worked. I could flick the flint to make flashes to guide me towards the source of the sound.

I stood up and inched my way through the blackness, flicking the lighter as I went. I walked fifteen feet then stubbed my foot on a large, soft object.

A HAUNTED POOL

Something was blocking the path. I flicked the lighter and – in the split second of light – saw something horrific.

A young deer lay slain across the path. It was on its side with its legs sprawled out; its neck was torn and bloody. Its eyes gazed lifelessly up at me. Blood was seeping across the ground and under my feet. I felt heat rising from the wound. What in the world could have done this? Clearly, there were things more terrifying than ghosts haunting this lake.

I stood there, unable to move, for an age. The tension in the air around me was unbearable – like slow strokes of a knife being sharpened on a stone. I yearned for company, for safety, for the sound of a distant motorcar to remind me that I was not totally alone.

How long? How long should I wait? How long before the predator pounces again? Should I stand motionless in the hope that I would survive the attentions of 'the beast' or should I make a dash for freedom, attempting to outrun the lightning strides and killer instinct of what must surely be a big cat?

If I was going to die, then I might as well die running. I ran as fast as I could, into the wood and towards the far side. I heard no bounding behind me, nothing clawed at my back. The wood thinned and I reached open fields. I had made it, unnerved but unscathed.

My experience at the Haunted Pool made me realise that 'lake atmosphere' is a clear communication from the lake to those who visit. The pool wasn't hostile. The discomfort I'd felt on previous trips, and the lack of fish on that fateful night, were – I believe – the lake's way of getting me to leave so that I'd make it home safely. That didn't make the experience any less eerie. I'd learnt that, when left alone with nothing but one's emotions and inner thoughts for company, the nocturnal world could be completely overpowering. A haunting of the mind in a world of night.

I still pity the deer, heading to the pool for a night-time drink, that saved me from the clutches of the beast.

1994

VI

THE MONASTERY POND

Waking in the comfort of my bedroom after a night at The Haunted Pool was like escaping from a troubled dream into the warm folds of normality. I opened my eyes gently, seeing sunlight streaming through a gap in the curtains, and felt relieved that I was safe, that morning had arrived to save me from the clutches of night. I pulled the blankets up over my head and thought, "It's okay, it was only a nightmare; go back to sleep." I lay there for a moment, then realised that it wasn't a dream at all.

The Haunted Pool had troubled my dreams for too long. There were many mornings when I woke to the sound of that feline scream echoing through my mind. I needed to change my emotional state. Another angling trip was needed, this time to somewhere lighter, airier, more relaxed and altogether more pleasant. Somewhere that would redress the balance and compensate for the chills that were numbing my bones.

My thoughts turned to a pool within cycling distance of home. It had an encouraging presence, like a bouncy castle at a child's party. I knew it contained carp, I'd seen

them there before. So I was soon out of bed and getting dressed, thinking of the fish that awaited me. I was at the lake within an hour.

At an acre-and-a-half, the lake was shaped like a flint arrowhead, its banks tapering into the distance where a stream entered the pool. It was bordered on the left bank by alders and oaks; and on the right bank by goat willow, ash and poplar. The land to the right of the lake sloped upwards towards the summit of a small hill, upon which I could see a single-storey building surrounded by a neatly clipped beech hedge. (I'd inspected the building before and concluded that it was the stable block to a large manor house.)

I chose to fish a swim on the northwest side of the pond, where the morning sun was warming the water. I'd seen some telltale bubbles emerging from the depths and the water appeared cloudy, as if it was the fishes' chosen place for breakfast. A willow overhung the water to my left and a bed of burr reed lined the margins to my right.

My bait for the trip was a small chunk of luncheon meat, fished over a bed of stewed hempseed. My favourite float – a swan quill with a fiery orange tip and black whippings – would register any bites. I could have chosen other floats, but this one seemed right for the occasion and was now sitting attentively in the water like a child awaiting a swimming lesson.

I noticed a cluster of bubbles break the surface near

to my float. The float dipped, wobbled, and then lay flat before gliding into the depths. An explosion of adrenaline saw me grab the rod and strike firmly into the fish. My float, which had been attached to the line with a rubber band, sprang free and flew over my shoulder into the vegetation behind me. A cloud of mud and bubbles bulged in the water as the carp bow-waved for freedom; my centrepin span furiously as the fish headed out into the lake. The speed and energy of the carp was startling, like holding on to a lightning rod in an electrical storm. It travelled twenty yards before I was able to clamp down on the reel and turn its head.

There is a moment during every fight with a strong fish when you wonder whether you will win the battle. Sometimes you are confident of your upper hand: you have stout tackle or open water in which to play the fish; other times you sense that the fish will never be yours. You may even be subjected to the anglers' curse, where the line will part or the hook pulls from the fish's mouth with no apparent reason. You simply have to reel in, check your knots and go through the whole experience again. Fortunately for me, the carp I'd hooked was succumbing to my efforts. My rod was absorbing its lunges and I was able to draw it steadily towards me, albeit with some violent thrashes and short runs prior to being drawn over the net.

Adrenaline turned to elation, then euphoria. The carp was landed. I lifted the net, with fish inside, from the water and placed it onto the grass at my feet. Through the mesh of the net I could see that the carp was a dark, old fish. Its scales looked more like polished bronze than gold. The metallic glints of the scales and the glistening, mesh-like texture of its flanks made it look like a gilded warrior lying defeated in the battlefield. Its golden-irised eye stared at me, and I back. The connection was made between captor and captive. I unhooked the fish, then carried it to the water's edge and released it into the depths. I waved my hat in salutation.

"Nice fish." The voice came from the top of the bank behind me. I looked up to see a slender man who, to my surprise, was wearing a dark blue monk's habit. He was holding a bible to his chest and gazing out across the lake. He tilted his head and looked to the sky, as if thanking God for this special place.

The man told me that his name was Nicholas and he was living in the building at the top of the hill. The building was, he revealed, a monastery. Franciscan monks had established it as a retreat house at the start of the last century. It was a House of God, available to people seeking an escape from their troubled lives. Brother Benedict was the guardian, overseeing proceedings, with six friars in assistance.

Nicholas told me that he was not a monk but one of the visitors benefiting from the monks' hospitality. Since arriving at the monastery, he had led a basic life.

He'd risen at six o'clock each morning for prayer and meditation; he'd then eat a simple, silent luncheon and, afterwards, partake of the Eucharist. His afternoons were his own where he would go for a contemplative stroll around the lake. He found the pool to be a spiritual and calming place. Never an angler, he asked what the appeal was to me. But before I could utter a response, he guessed that it was, fundamentally, the same as drew him to the pool each day. "We have a calling, don't we?" he said, "A need to be close to nature, where water may cleanse our souls and wash away the stresses of yesterday. It is emotional recompense for the cost of living."

A clock bell rang in the monastery tower. It was time for Nicholas to go to prayer. We said our goodbyes. I couldn't help but feel envious of his simple existence – the uncluttered lifestyle, daily routine and ultra-slow pace of living.

As Nicholas turned to go, he said, "Life's a simple thing; it's we who insist on making it complicated."

I looked towards the lake. Would my prayers be answered? Would it be a day of simple pleasures? Possibly, if I could find that wretched float.

Unbeknown to me, things were happening elsewhere that would change my fishing forever. My quest for wild carp, and the traditional angling I was practicing, was about to take me on a long, long journey, far away from home.

1995

VII

A TRIP TO THE SHOPS

On 13th March 1995, the British Government did something that pleased many but appalled a minority: they abolished the coarse fishing closed season on stillwaters. The public explanation was that it benefitted fishery owners whose livelihoods depended on angling, and that public consensus was that it would be a good thing. Most lakes, reservoirs and canals (those not designated a Site of Special Scientific Interest) could now be fished year-round so that 'the industry' could benefit from increased revenues and, if you viewed things cynically, the Government could collect more taxes from angling-related sales. In my opinion, the move defied the needs of nature (fish need a rest from anglers so that they can spawn in peace). It was a commercial sell-out. To many, the decision marked a regression, where anglers were moving away from their reputation as custodians of nature. Now, coarse anglers could fish all year round, including the time of year when fish are most sensitive: spawning time. Somehow, the obvious became overlooked: that it is wrong to knowingly interfere with a creature when its physical condition is most vulnerable. Unfortunately for fish welfare, it is the time of year when female fish – laden with spawn – are heaviest. Biggest is best, right?

The three month closed season – that ran from 15th March to 15th June inclusive – had existed since 1923 to protect coarse fish at the time of year when they needed shelter; it also helped to keep the balance in an angler's life. For it is not healthy to fish all year round, at least not for the same species or even at the same venue. Angling – indeed life – is enriched by the diversity it can offer and so the closed season forced anglers to widen their horizons, to do other things, such as fish for game fish (trout and salmon have a different closed season to coarse fish), fish in the sea, fish abroad, or – salvation – not fish at all. The latter would see anglers enjoying a normal life, at home with their families, or escaping to the lakeside to bait up a swim or to enjoy a pre-season work party. Whatever they chose, doing so ensured that their excitement would peak at midnight on 16th June.

The 'Glorious 16th', as it was known, was an important date for the traditional wildie fisher; carp being an archetypal summer species. In 1995 this ritual was potentially shattered by the Government's decision to allow coarse anglers to fish stillwaters throughout the spring. There was now a realistic chance that you'd arrive at your chosen lake only to find the vegetation flattened, fish sulking, and an angler fishing in your chosen spot.

A TRIP TO THE SHOPS

Fortunately for me, there was a water in southern England, called Jade Lake, where the syndicate had vowed to keep the traditional closed season. In glorious defiance to the perceived opinion of the masses, its members had abstained from fishing and were looking forward to the 16th with more enthusiasm than ever. The spring months had been mild, the fish had already spawned and recovered, and the pre-baited pitches were rumoured to be alive with feeding fish. Because of this, this year's 16th June at Jade was destined to be the best-ever start to the season. Thanks to my passion for traditional angling, and correspondence with a certain Chris Yates (the grand-master of traditional angling), I'd secured a place on the syndicate.

There was no way that I was going to miss the event. The 16th of June was the most special and eagerly awaited day in my fishing year. I would arrive on the 15th, walk the banks looking for fish, and savour the sights and sounds of wildlife that had been left undisturbed for three months. I'd settle into a chosen swim, throw some bait into the water to give the fish confidence, then sit back and await the turn of midnight before casting in. There was only one problem with my plan: Jade Lake was much further afield than my normal waters. Being 21 and 'a little late off the starting blocks' with my driving lessons, I hadn't yet passed my driving test.

I imagine that sixty miles doesn't sound far to a car driver? (This is how far I would have to travel from my Berkshire cottage to Jade Lake.) Perhaps an hour if traffic was clear? But I couldn't drive. Perhaps I could walk there? Laden with the tackle and bait for several days' fishing, I calculated that it would take five days. Then there would be the return journey to undertake with blisters and aching legs. With only a week's holiday booked from work, walking was out of the question. There was, however, a third option.

I'd recently started work as a gardener on a large country estate at Lambourn near Newbury. Upon appointment, the Lady of the Manor acknowledged that, as I couldn't drive, I was potentially stranded within the estate grounds. To solve the issue, she had offered me the use of her bicycle to 'nip to the shops'. I'd since accepted her offer, using the bike to fetch groceries from the nearby town of Hungerford, so she was accustomed to seeing me remove it from the stable yard. The only question was: 'would she miss the bike for a week?' Fortunately for me, the Lady of the Manor was on holiday throughout June.

The bicycle was one of those small-wheeled ladies bikes – not dissimilar to a folding travel bike – with a wicker basket at the front and only three gears. It was painted a cerise-burgundy colour and had garish white tyres that looked like they'd come straight from the set of Happy Days. Thankfully, there were no pink tassels on the handlebars to draw further attention to me whilst riding it. Aesthetics aside, the bike was far from

A TRIP TO THE SHOPS

Fit for 60 miles and a hundredweight of tackle and bait?

functional. It didn't have a crossbar to which I would strap my rods, and was so small that my knees would hit the handlebar if I attempted to sit down on the saddle. In its favour, the bike did have a wire pannier over the rear wheel that could support a creel and bait bucket.

Cycling it would be. With my transport selected, I was good to go. I would make it to the lake for the 16th even if I had to set out before dawn on the 15th and ride into the night with no lights to guide me. Which is exactly what I did.

Rising at 3am, on the day before the fishing season begins, may seem like a rude disturbance to a good night's sleep. But I hadn't slept; I couldn't. There was no need for an alarm clock. The adrenaline running through me ensured that I was already awake and doing my best not to jump up and down on my bed like a hyperactive trampolinist. In truth, I had lain there for an hour awaiting the 'departure time'. But at 3am, it was time to leave.

I'd prepared all my tackle and bait the previous night, arranging it in a neat pile in the centre of my living room. There was a rod holdall containing two rods, a landing net and an umbrella; a 75-litre rucksack containing a change of clothes (in case I fell in), food, water, wine and port, a camera, binoculars, stove, gas canisters and saucepans; a wicker creel containing two reels, spare line, shot, legers and hooks, candles, tealeaves, teapot, china mug, sketchbook, writing pad and pens, catapult and collection of lucky acorns; a large bait bucket containing fifteen pounds of cooked hempseed, ten pounds of cooked tiger nuts, five pounds of chum mixers, four cans of sweetcorn, two loaves of crusty bread, two tins of luncheon meat and a small pot of worms; finally there was a Kelly Kettle, and a wax jacket that looked like a scarecrow because its arms were stuffed with newspaper for kindling.

Not much, then, to load onto my bike and lug sixty miles. It was only when carrying the gear through my front door to the bicycle that I realised just how much kit I was proposing to take. How on earth would I transport all this? My knees buckled as I attempted to lift the rucksack onto my back. The week's supply of food and water was too much. Some of it had to go. Not wishing to scrimp on the food, I decided that my supply of water, which filled a three-gallon container, would have to be poured away and that a supply would need to be found closer to the lake. Even so, I guessed that the remaining cargo weighed nearly a hundredweight.

I tied the bait bucket to the pannier with baling twine borrowed from the farmyard on the estate. My creel was tied to the top of the bucket and my Kelly Kettle dangled loosely on the side. Given that the bike had no crossbar, I ended up strapping my rod holdall to the frame on the left hand side of each wheel. It was secure, but I wouldn't be able to turn left. So at each junction or corner, I would have to stop, lift the front wheel and shuffle it towards the desired direction of travel.

I locked the front door and, with my rucksack digging into my shoulders, set forth into the night. I opted to walk the bike for the first half-mile, to allow everything to bed down and to check that the tyres could withstand the weight. And then I was off. I mounted the bike and pushed forwards. Everything held. I gripped the handlebars tightly and whizzed down country lanes pocketed with mist that concealed bottom-jarring potholes and startled-looking muntjac deer. The sun had not yet risen, though there was a faint glow forming behind me on the eastern horizon. I was heading west, on a marathon bike ride from Berkshire to deepest Wiltshire. One pedal, one hill, at a time.

The rod holdall strapped to the side of the bike made for very cumbersome cycling. Not only could I not turn left, I could only pedal if I angled my left knee out as far as possible and pressed down with the heel of my foot. I soon mastered the technique and after a mile or so was reaching speeds equivalent to a hot-rodded milk float, albeit in a clunky, awkward fashion.

The journey felt lonely as I passed through Bagshot and Shelbourne. There was not a sign of life, not even a dawn chorus in the treetops. I rested at the brow of a steep hill at Wexcombe. The landscape here reminded me of proper 'BB country' and was reminiscent of his cover illustration to The Quiet Fields. The views from here across the North Wessex Downs were fabulous, allowing me to survey the wide panorama and see a burning copper sun melting the horizon. It was going to be a hot day, not especially ideal for cycling in corduroy trousers, wellies and a tweed jacket.

The road down and across the downs, via Cadley and Everleigh, was much easier, being mostly downhill. I guessed I was about half way. The small map that I had in my pocket was not to be trusted – it said I had only done a third of the journey, yet I was feeling the strain so it must have been further.

It was mid-morning when I reached the Upper Avon valley and the village of Fittleton. I'd been travelling for several hours and so decided to stop near the bridge over the Avon and read a two-month-old newspaper that I'd rolled up and stuffed inside my wax jacket.

I continued through Netheravon and across Enford Down, enjoying avoiding the main roads and traffic noise. The road here was more like a dirt track and the ground was mostly grassland interspersed with gorse and stands of pine trees. I heard the familiar song of a skylark overhead and so stopped to see if I could spot it, but it was too high in the sky. I was then nearly knocked over by a deafening boom that rocked the valley, making the ground shudder and the handlebar of my bike wobble uncontrollably. The noise had come from less than three hundred yards away. From beyond the nearby pines came a huge cloud of black smoke and a squeaking, rumbling sound that sounded worryingly like the caterpillar tracks of a tank. I looked back at my map. I'd strayed from my intended course and entered a military 'Danger Area', where, it seemed, there were tanks firing live ammunition. Lifting my front wheel, I did a super-quick 'three-sixty' and pushed down with all my might on the right pedal. The rutted, gravel track made for a real boneshaker of a ride, but I pedalled for my life, passing the signs and red flags and wooden barricades that I'd overlooked earlier. I was shaking and hyperventilating when I reached a proper road again, vowing to look up when cycling rather than keeping my eyes focused on the roads and potholes six feet in front of me.

As I headed back over the River Avon, the gently swaying weed in the river helped to calm my state. And then I chuckled; I'd put my life on the line for the 16th June. No one could ever accuse me of not doing my bit for tradition. Though, if I had been blown to pieces by a canon shell, I wonder what the military coroner would have made of a pair of smoking wellies and a hundred yard scattering of hempseed, tiger nuts and sweetcorn?

The following miles were a blur; I was just glad to be alive. Strangely, in my dazed state, all I could think about was the furious punishment that the Lady of the Manor would have given me if the Ministry of Defence had destroyed her bike. My likely explanation? "Seems I bought too much Russian vodka from the shops."

I passed by Stonehenge and through Amesbury high street, finally waking from my daze as I battled up a gruelling hill near Upper Woodford. My legs were turning to jelly, the heel of my left foot felt like nails had been driven into it from the miles of pedalling, and my spine felt shredded from the weight of the rucksack. I had to dismount the bicycle, remove my rucksack and place it over the bike's handlebars, then push everything up the hill, cursing under my breath as I made each agonising step. I reached the top of the hill after thirty minutes, feeling like a mountaineer who had reached the peak of the mountain only to realise, in a moment of

A TRIP TO THE SHOPS

muscle-trembling exhaustion, that he was but halfway through his journey.

I opted to rest, to ease my aches and improve my mood. Today was a day to celebrate, not be beaten by exhaustion, so a 'brunch stop' by the side of the road would be a good idea. I leant my bike against a roadside hedge and sat upon a rickety old wooden stile that had seemingly assisted the journeys of thousands of travellers before.

My stop was one of happy contemplation and excitement. All the wondrous journeys made by anglers in seasons past, their hopes high and their minds filled with thoughts of dawn mists, twitching floats, battles with large fish, and the calm that comes from time spent beside water. I refused to dwell on thoughts of those who had lobbied for the abolition of the closed season on stillwaters, reassuring myself that river anglers would at least be feeling the usual sense of jubilation as they headed to flowing water on the 'Glorious 16th'. How many anglers, I wondered, would be plotting to free up time to fish on this special day? How many children would be bunking off school? How many workers would be phoning in sick? How many people would end up sitting beside the water, knowing that this was the most special day in the coarse fisher's calendar? Thousands, if not millions, of anglers would be venturing forward tomorrow, with hopes lifted by the prospect of a magical new season.

Thinking of calendars and opportunities to indulge one's pleasures, I realised it was time for lunch. I reached into my rucksack and brought out my usual gardener's meal of Cornish pasty, Stilton cheese, a crusty wholemeal roll, radishes, celery, hardboiled egg, a packet of crisps, a caramel wafer bar, and a flask of tea. So tasty, and my rucksack would be lighter afterwards.

Replenished from the meal, I straddled the bike, pushed forward, and hurtled down the far side of the hill. I was determined not to use my brakes and so took a number of precarious 'high lean' left-hand bends at speed, avoiding oncoming cars, a stray cow and even overtaking an ultra-keen cyclist dressed in a strange, stretchy, fluorescent yellow outfit, who looked at me in disbelief as I whooshed by, whooping for joy.

A bridge over the beautiful River Wylye marked the bottom of the hill. Clear, deep waters of the river below were carpeted with flowering water crowfoot; riverside houses looked lost in time; and adjacent fields were a sea of shimmering blue linseed flowers, which blended into a haze where they met the azure blue sky on the horizon. It lifted my heart and caused me to pause and stake stock, being grateful that places like this still existed.

It was a fine day for gazing, but not for cycling. The mid-day heat was well into the eighties and there wasn't a breath of wind. Perspiration was running down my brow and into my eyes, stinging as it did and making me wonder whether it was time to remove my tweed jacket. I did so, tying its arms around the creel and bucket on the pannier behind me.

The road between Great Wishford and Wylye ran parallel to a railway line and the river, so was lovely and flat – just what I needed after fifty miles of endless pedalling. This slower, more relaxed, style of cycling was more to my taste. I was able to sit on the saddle, straighten my back and lift my chin; whilst, of course, keeping my left knee jutted outwards and pushing down on the pedal with the heel of my foot. The slower speed also meant that I was more aware of the sounds and scents around me. Which was worrying.

It came to my attention that the bike was beginning to creak under the weight of its cargo and that the chain, now virtually devoid of oil, was squeaking like a shrew on its wedding night. My poor old corduroy trousers, which were drenched in sweat, were rubbing against my rod holdall with each turn of the pedal, creating a dull rasping 'vroop-vroop' sound. My creel was also creaking and the Kelly Kettle was clonking against the bait bucket like a cowbell. To make matters worse, the heat had caused my tiger nuts to start fermenting. Consequently, my bait bucket was making 'impolite' flatulent noises. It was bubbling away and, due to an imperfect seal on the bucket, was releasing frequent wafts of yeasty aroma that sounded like I'd had too many beans for breakfast. No wonder the cyclist I'd just seen had looked at me in disbelief. Together, the noises of the bike, trousers, creel, Kelly Kettle and fermenting bait bucket must have sounded like workshop of a mad inventor. Cycling faster made it worse. The 'clunk-clunk, eek-eeeek, vroop-vroop, creeeaw, clonk, gugger-gugger…PAAARP!' got louder and faster with each turn of the pedal.

As I passed through the Langfords, the villagers standing in front of their cottages looked baffled as they saw and heard this eccentric cyclist wheezing through their high street in the heat of the day, left leg angled out, piloting a two-wheeled contraption that sounded like it ought to have been blueprinted in a Heath Robinson cartoon. It was laughable and a little embarrassing, but it mattered not. I was getting close to my destination.

With less than ten miles to go, I forged onwards, up and over a mountainous hill between Wylye and Dinton and along the Nadder valley. Distinctive creamy-grey limestone buildings and walling marked that I was getting close to my Wiltshire destination and then, as I began my descent into the final valley, I saw my first glimpse of the lake. It seemed to extend for miles upon miles, its size accentuated by the shimmering heat haze. It's waters blurring into a mist of jade, ultramarine, olive and bronze.

After nine hours and sixty miles of cycling, I was in sight of the lake. 'The' lake. The one where its anglers had defied the wishes of the Government and

would honour the old season. I was proudly one of them, doing everything I could to remain traditional. My cycling efforts had made the dream become real. I prayed that the new season would reward me with a wildie on opening night.

I rolled down a grassy field that led to the water's edge, halting alongside a nettle-fringed fence that ran beneath a line of alders. All I had to do was get off the bike and my journey would be complete. However, my first wobbly footfall onto solid earth was a disaster. My leg gave way beneath me and I collapsed into the nettles; my bike and luggage tumbled down on top of me, soaking me in sticky tiger nut syrup and bruising my already aching body. With nettles stinging my hands and face, I pushed at the ground beneath me and clambered at the fence above, attempting to stand up. I couldn't. I was devoid of energy. My legs were cramped and numb, my lungs were burning and my backside felt like it had received 'six of the best' from the headmaster's cane. Yet I felt overwhelmingly elated. I had made it: to this wonderful, special, traditional, lake. I lay there laughing, wondering how and if I could get back up again. I'd make it up eventually, but for now was content to lie in my stinging, sticky, uncomfortable bed of nettles, bait and bike.

My 'trip to the shops' had been more than a journey of miles; it was a feat of endurance, of resolve to fish in traditional ways and enjoy something precious that an apparent majority no longer valued. The bicycle had done me proud but was in a terribly abused state. The previously white tyres were now black, their treads worn away by the miles of scalding tarmac. My bait bucket was dripping snot-like gloop onto my trousers, the inner thighs of which were bald of corduroy from rubbing against my holdall. It didn't matter. The journey was worth it. Today was the 15th June. And tomorrow, tomorrow was the most important date of the year: the first day of the fishing season.

1995

VIII

AMONGST THE SECRET CARP

Waking on the 16th June to the song of a blackbird in an alder overhead was as if Nature herself was encouraging me to rise and savour the delights of a summer dawn. It was the start of the new season, one that had arrived as if with special presence for those who had abstained from fishing until this day.

The season started for me at midnight with a token cast into the inky gloom, a distant and subtle 'plop' as the bait entered the water, a clicking of a reel as I tightened the line and then a slurp of tea from a china cup as I relaxed and cherished the moment. The night was cold; there was even a light dusting of frost in the meadow behind the trees. I'd not had the foresight to bring a sleeping bag, blanket, or matress, so I'd curled up under my wax jacket and endured the nocturnal chill.

Four hours passed and, with no signs of carp to keep me awake, I'd eventually succumbed to the world of sleep. But now the day was beginning. Through the half-light I could see the faint shapes of trees opposite. A dawn mist was swirling up from the water and condensing on my clothes like the tears of a lost season.

Given my excitement and efforts to be here, I had expected to be fishing intensively; but I was not. Actually, there was no urgency to recast or move to a different spot, and no immediate desire to catch a fish. The moment and the sense of place were overwhelming. I primed my Kelly Kettle with twigs and paper, lit the kindling and as the plumes of smoke rose, sat back to contemplate the fortunes of this special place.

Jade Lake was once the playground of England's wealthiest man; a man ostracised by eighteenth century society to live in eccentric seclusion in his vast country estate. As if to snub his peers, he had obsessed with displaying his wealth via flamboyant architectural and materialistic excesses at the estate, building a vast abbey and designing a majestic parkland of woodland, lakes and meadows. His vision grew with gothic and occasionally dark inspiration. Trees were planted close together to ensure a dark and cloistered air within the woods and the estate was filled with sculptures and grottoes. It became six thousand acres of secluded, excessive and indulgent perfection. At its centre was the abbey, a towering building designed by James Wyatt in the same style as the Houses of Parliament. Its tower was a third the height of Salisbury cathedral. A vast serpentine lake was constructed nearby. At over a mile long and lined with rare trees and unusual follies, the pool was champion of the statuesque.

Depending on your viewpoint, what happened next was either travesty or destiny. The owner's quest for perfection, and obsession with greatness, drove him to build such an extravagant estate that it caused its own undoing. The once limitless budget dried up and, facing bankruptcy, the owner sold the estate. Shortly after, the great abbey collapsed leaving only the parkland as testament to the genius of its creator. The follies began to crumble; the woodland matured and began to fall. Once-manicured laurels, box and yew became entwined in a wild jungle that sprouted up; the grottoes became hidden beneath a thicket of scrub vegetation. The gates to the estate were locked and the immense walls that surrounded it were eventually concealed beneath miles upon miles of sprawling ivy. Jade became a lost kingdom.

The lake, as if in defiance to the passing of time, blossomed. Isolated and untouched for two hundred years, it was able to mature, grow weedy and silty and to develop a mysticism that only old lakes can achieve. Its sixty acres of almost turquoise waters remained unfished. It had once held carp and perch and there were reputed to be large trout, but that was two hundred years earlier. The years in between had settled to create a stratum of myths and monsters. It would just take the right angler, a worthy angler, to unlock this mystery and connect with the past.

And there was I, making a cup of tea.

I can't lay claim to discovering Jade, or unlocking the first of its mysteries (these were described by Chris Yates in his book *The Secret Carp*), but being there had a profound influence on my perception of the angling ideal.

Fishing at Jade made me realise how effectively Nature tends to her own. This was once an environment created for the whims of Man. The estate may once have been great but now, with the assistance of Nature, it was greater still: wilder, more ancient, foreboding and exciting. Man's attempts for domination over Nature had collapsed spectacularly beneath the might of time. Jade was a wilderness punctuated with gothic statues and huge parkland trees, remnants of a vision gone to seed. It was a playground for the soul, freedom for the mind and a wilderness to explore. Being there, I felt less like an angler and more like an explorer.

There were others on the exploration. Like-minded anglers immersed in the lake's character and history, pursuing an archaeological quest with rod and line, tunnelling through the undergrowth to come face-to-face with an exciting discovery: a fallen ruin, a ritualistic altar, a secret cave or grotto, a magnificent golden carp.

Being the 16th June, there were a number of these 'exploring' anglers at the lake, each of whom spotted the smoke signal from my Kelly Kettle. They emerged from the undergrowth like water voles escaping a flood. They were new acquaintances, soon to be friends, joined by

a bond to fish in traditional ways and continue the lore of the new season.

I knew the first two anglers – Chris Yates and Mick 'Demus' Canning – as I'd fished with them before. Indeed, my two-year correspondence with Chris had resulted in him proposing me for membership of the Jade syndicate. Mick, with whom I'd fished for wildies before, was one of the most successful catchers of big barbel of the Hampshire Avon. The remaining anglers – Richard Battersby, Jon Berry and Jeff Greene – were new to me and to the syndicate, but I could tell from their floppy hats and weatherworn tweeds that they were old school traditional anglers and countrymen like me.

We made our introductions, then sat and talked. As the teapot stewed over the embers of the Kelly, we shared a brew and discussed the events of the preceding night. Chris had caught an eight-pound wildie from his swim near the corner of the dam, Jeff had eaten an entire fruitcake, Jon had connected with a carp that pulled him into the lake, and somewhere, somehow, several bottles of port had been emptied. We blamed Richard.

Talk soon switched to the clapped-out bicycle propped up near the alders. Apparently, the smell from its smoking tyres had cloaked the more natural nighttime scents. I owned up to the offence and told the story of how I'd got there. We celebrated my madness with another cup of tea.

Chris and Mick were the most familiar with Jade, having fished there in seasons' past. They relayed the folklore of the water and said that, although wildies were present, there were other leviathan fish lurking in the deeps that could haunt a man's dreams for a lifetime. "Great carp so large as to make you think twice before casting in," said Mick. "Huge, never-before-caught fish," said Chris, "that, if hooked, would pull so hard that they would terrify you into submission…unless, of course, you held your composure and landed a new record." They informed us that an angler had lowered his hookbait into the water beneath his rod tip only to hook one of these aqueous beasts, which proceeded to swim strongly and steadily across the breadth of the lake before smashing the line against a sunken tree on the far bank, some two hundred yards away. The angler had pulled with all his might but, for fear of his line parting, had been forced into a position of spectatorship as the fish emptied his reel of line.

Jon and Jeff were impressed, I gasped in awe, but Richard suggested that it was Chris and Mick who'd polished off the port and were suffering delusions.

Of course, we all knew that anglers' tales are just that and that the one that got away is always the biggest fish. But there was something about this lake – it's grandeur and mystery – that made it possible for this story to be true. Fortunately, none of us had joined the syndicate because of rumoured monsters. Chris had already caught a record carp so had nothing to prove; we had all fallen in love with the timeless scenery of the lake, the forbidden yew-shrouded islands and, of course, the preservation of the closed season. And besides, we would be more than content to catch wildies. It was with this vision imprinted on our minds that we set forth from our base camp, each with a rod in hand and carrying a small tub of bait, to stalk the overgrown margins for our opening day carp.

It would be a classic season.

1996

IX

CHASING MOLLIES

Being at Jade was a relaxed, tranquil, leisurely affair, like a well filling slowly after a long drought. Fishing was always on the agenda, but it wasn't really a priority; the lake was just so fabulously alluring. Like an attractive woman sitting at an easel and creating a beautiful masterpiece, Jade had an ability to charm and hypnotise her suitors. Days could be spent exploring the estate, venturing into the lost wood, delving into caves, or uncovering hidden obelisks and statues. They were exciting, innocent, times. We would make camps and dens, play hide and seek, climb trees or even just lie in the long grass whilst reading a favourite book. As much fun was had chasing lizards, or throwing popcorn to the trout in the overflow stream, as would be had in fishing. In autumn, we would be found collecting acorns, conkers and pinecones, or pressing colourful leaves into our angling diaries. It was an existence more akin to childhood years than men in their twenties, thirties and forties.

Angling was mostly confined to the summer and autumn months, which was when the lake was at her best. The angling approach was simple: just one rod, a centrepin reel, a net and a creel, with the bait freelined or fished beneath a quill float. We would stalk up and down the overgrown banks during the day, watching and learning the habits of the fish and lake's wildlife. It was social, team-style fishing where discoveries were freely shared and no secrets were kept. We all had a common purpose: to piece together Jade's unique puzzle and understand her moods, so that we might enjoy our time there even more. There was never any pressure to catch, we knew that Jade was a big lake and that the fun of fishing there was in the discoveries we made, not the successes we achieved.

Every now and then we would spot a carp, or sometimes a shoal of fish, swimming along the margins of the lake. They would glide through fallen snags or appear from beneath beds of lilies; sometimes they would appear as bow waves cutting through the silty shallows. Catching them wasn't easy, but we were confident of hooking at least one fish per trip. The carp were nearly all wildies: natural fish, born in the lake and ignorant (to the point of ignoring) any artificial bait that was presented to them. Consequently, simple baits such as maggots and worms were best, although hempseed, black-eyed beans, maple peas and tiger nuts were also effective.

At nightfall, we would return to base camp to socialise, eat and sleep. These nocturnal locations consisted of a

CHASING MOLLIES

Making camp before the other anglers arrive.

Looking for wildies amongst the fallen trees.

circle of sleeping bags and either umbrellas or canvas tents around a campfire; our lines would be cast out into the water with our rods in a neat line where we could see them. The routine was always the same: withdraw from the lake, meet up with other anglers, exchange stories, share cups of tea and enjoy an evening meal. As we retired to our sleeping bags each night, we would thank Jade for being so generous.

Jade, it seemed, was the perfect host, a warm and welcoming spirit. But it hadn't always been like this. Our treasured pool harboured a dark secret.

In the distant past, not long after the ill-fated abbey had been completed, a terrible deed had occurred in the woods at the rear of the lake. The screams of a young woman had been heard, followed by a deafening silence that lasted for days.

Local legend told of a dark, stormy night, when a fierce wind tore through the woods and rain fell like rods of lead. A cry had been heard from within the walls of the abbey; two figures had emerged dressed in black, carrying a kicking and writhing sack upon their shoulders. They threw the bundle into an awaiting carriage and galloped at breakneck speed into the depths of the woods. The sound of horses' hooves echoed across the valley.

The horses galloped for two miles, to a point high above the lake. There, in a clearing in the forest, they came to a halt, their backs bloody from the relentless whipping by the enraged carriage man.

The sack was flung from the carriage and dragged into the centre of the clearing, where there stood an altar made from carved limestone. Rain poured down its engraved facades and pooled at its base as if the ground itself were weeping. The fabric of the sack was torn open to reveal a petrified young woman dressed in a white nightgown, her brown hair platted and her pale face contorted with fear. She was a housemaid at the abbey and her name was Molly.

Molly was the most loving and cheerful of all the staff at the abbey. She had befriended the owner and, it was rumoured, was with child. The scandal could not be made public, so her fate was sealed. Her body was never found, but the blood that soaked into the soft limestone of the altar had revealed her sinister fate.

Molly and her unborn baby had perished upon the altar that night, but legend claimed that their spirits had lived on; such was Molly's love for life and her joy in seeing beauty in all things. The eerie silence of the woods began to ease and life in the forest increased tenfold. Birdsong could be heard at new levels, glow-worms abounded and carp could be seen leaping in the great lake whose shores fringed the woods. Molly's presence could be felt everywhere, even in the darkest realms of the forest. She was alive in all things, things that became known as the Mollies of Jade Lake.

Two hundred years later, the altar still remained,

its weathered stone looking up at the sky as if seeking forgiveness for a past deed. The clearing in the wood, however, was the most peaceful place on the whole estate, its floor was carpeted in bluebells and wild garlic and the surrounding trees ensured that the place was always sheltered and warm. It was a place of serenity.

The first time I discovered the altar, I had been venturing deep into the woods, tracking a roe deer that had been out grazing in daylight. Stumbling into the clearing, I noticed the grey slab of stone and was instantly reminded of the legend. I stood there in bewilderment until, from the corner of my eye, I saw two blue butterflies dancing merrily in a ray of sunlight.

I stood there for a while, watching the playful butterflies, then said: "Hello Molly, I'm glad to make your acquaintance." Though, of course, I knew that only one of them was Molly; the other was her child, happy to be fluttering in the sunlight with his or her mother.

This experience typified the warm and inviting nature of Jade. It was a magical place, where happy goings-on were gifted by one less fortunate. If Jade's spirit had a human presence, then it would wrap its arms around you and protect you. Its name, was Molly.

1997

X

DOUBLE VISION

Into the Unknown

All lakes have secrets. Some are subtle and some are ridiculous; some are never known. Large lakes such as Jade can hold onto their mysteries forever. Other lakes have a mischievous streak and occasionally hint at their secrets, but their fickle mood ensures they are never fully explained.

Anglers love unlocking a lake's secrets. It is a desire bred out of continual taunting by the lake, a playground chant of 'I know something that you don't know'. Because of this, carp lakes can become mesmerising.

What of the secrets themselves? Do they even know of their clandestine nature? And what might these secrets be? In the watery world of ancient lakes, the greatest mystery, the forbidden secret, is often the presence of a gigantic fish. A fish so abnormally large, old and cunning that it is beyond belief. Even if it is nothing more than a rumour, the concept of greatness is enough to give birth to the myth, that there is an emperor amongst the legions of lesser carp.

Some say that sufficient probing will reveal all but the most shielded secret. People, they intimate, are weak and can be broken. Lakes, however, are different. You have to earn their trust through faithful and frequent worship. But this requires a conscious pursuit, a willingness to probe, and a desire to know the secret in the first place. Not all of us have the inclination or motivation to unlock such tightly held secrets. For some, the presence of a myth is better than a myth made real; a quest into the unknown is more dramatic than following a well-trodden path.

A lake should always have secrets...

A Call in the Night

My dreams of monster carp were swimming strongly when, from the darkness of my cottage, came a harsh and abrupt sound. It was the phone ringing. I rose from bed and checked the clock in the hall. It said 11.30pm. I answered the telephone and was greeted by an excited voice, saying: "Are you sitting down? Tell me you are sitting down, you must be sitting down!" The voice barely paused for breath.

"Yes, I'm sitting down. In fact, I was recently in bed. Lying down. Horizontal. Asleep. Unable to fall over."

"Good, then I must tell you of the vision. The double vision!" The voice stressed the word 'double' as if one vision was no longer adequate.

"Okay, enlighten me."

"Demus and I were exploring at Jade Lake this afternoon, working our way up the east bank, beyond the grotto. We had shuffled along on hands and knees beneath an enormous laurel bush. In the middle of it we found an opening that led right down to the water's edge. The water wasn't deep there; we could see clean gravel on the bottom, where all around was silty. Fish were close by, we could feel it. The swim was framed by large snags either side – mature beech trees that that had fallen parallel to each other into the water. We knew we were looking at a classic carp swim, one that had never-before been fished. It was our discovery, somewhere worth investigating with rod and line."

The voice continued, "We just knelt there, behind a fringe of rushes that lined the water's edge, looking out into the water. Observing, hoping. Demus saw the first fish, a dark shadowy shape gliding in from left to right. But the light wasn't quite right; the glare of the sun was preventing us from seeing the fish fully. So we shifted our weight onto our feet and slowly rose up from behind the rushes so that we could gaze down into the water. There, not ten feet from where we stood, was a huge fish. An astounding fish. A fully scaled carp, slate grey-and-bronze in colour, with palm-sized pectoral fins that wafted the gravels for signs of food. It was in only four feet of water and yet the surface did not shift or bulge. The carp poised for a moment and we were able to assess its total size. It was immense, easily bigger than anything I've caught before. A genuine king of kings.'

"That's amazing, astounding," I replied, "so why aren't you there fishing for it?"

"Wait, I've not finished," cried the voice, "when you hear what I have to say you'll understand why I'm not fishing and have, instead, returned home for a strong drink."

"Sorry, please continue."

"Demus and I stood there in astonishment, marvelling at this wondrous creature, when the unexpected and unbelievable happened: another carp of equal size to the first appeared from the snag to our left and swam alongside its twin. The revelation, that there were *two* monsters in this lake, both of stupendous *record breaking* proportions, both capable of changing someone's world forever, was unfathomable."

The voice continued, "We could barely comprehend the implications of this vision – this double vision – that we'd stumbled upon. Such enormous fish, such intoxicating presence, such torment. We were frozen, unable to speak, unable to think of anything other than these two great fish. And then, as quickly as they arrived, they departed, leaving nothing more than a stunned silence and an image that will haunt our dreams. We had to come home. It was too much, too great an image for us to comprehend."

"So that's why you rang me, to share the burden?"

"No, to tell you that you and I are going fishing there tomorrow. No questions. Just bring your strongest tackle!"

The phone went dead and I was left alone with my thoughts, recounting what I'd just heard. The voice had been that of my friend Chris Yates, the man who, until two years earlier, was the British carp record holder. He had just seen two uncaught common carp that would have beaten his fifty-one pound best, whose only thought when returning home was to ring me to tell me the news and who – like me – would probably be unable to sleep until after he and I had fished together for these great creatures.

I'd heard plenty of stories before, in fact every carp lake I'd ever fished had its resident monster myth, a freakish story designed to keep carp anglers from their beds on nights such as this. But this story had credibility. Chris was more than qualified to assess the size of a large carp. "Bigger than anything I've caught before." His words continued to ring in my head. Could these fish really be bigger than his record? Bigger than a fifty-one pounder? Not one fish but two. The biggest brace of carp in the land? Two fish witnessed by two very experienced anglers. An image each; a vision to share; a dual message. A double vision.

Yes, these fish were real. The sighting had proved the legend of mighty carp living in Jade's deeps, rod-wrenching leviathans that could pull a man to his feet. But they had never been seen before, until now.

Rising to the Challenge

Being a pursuer of wild carp, and very much a poor gardener who mostly had to 'make do' with tackle I could make or find, my 'strongest tackle' was exactly the same as for all my other fishing: a nine foot split cane rod made from parts sourced from the attic of my local fishing tackle shop; a second-hand Dave Swallow centrepin, and a bamboo-poled landing net that I'd bought from a car boot sale. I'd never felt the urge, nor had the opportunity, to fish for huge carp, so my tackle had always proved adequate. I no longer had this luxury. I stared at my old bamboo rod. It was the hybrid love child of a MKIV Avon and a Sharpe's Scottie spinning rod; it had a permanent bend caused by a large barbel and would double over when battling anything over eight pounds. What if it actually hooked one of these record beasts? The rod would splinter like a toothpick. Who was I kidding? My muscles were willing but my tackle was feeble. The only item that gave me confidence was my Swallow centrepin, currently holding six-pound line but which, if loaded for something bold like *fifteen pounds* breaking strain line could – if I played the fish carefully – be capable of subduing the largest of carp.

Tackle or not, I would do this. I abandoned all thoughts of sleep and instead threw my clothes on top of my pyjamas and headed to the garden shed to prepare my fishing tackle.

I loaded my reel with the heavier line, then threaded the wiry coils through the rings of my rod and tested it by pulling against a sack of potatoes. It held, though I was astounded at the weight on the end. The twenty-kilo sack was about the same as the carp I was aspiring to catch. How could I pull such a heavy fish towards me, when it would be using all its strength to pull in the opposite direction? I returned to my cottage, grabbed two pillows from the bed, returned to the

shed and stuffed them into my net. They fitted, just. Big enough, then, to accommodate a carp that could be nearly four feet long. With my confidence lifted, I felt like a proper specimen hunter.

My plan was simple: hook first and panic later.

The Adventure Begins

It was 4am before I had loaded all my gear onto my bicycle, 5am before I had cycled to the local train station and 6am before I boarded the train from Reading to the southwest. My fellow passengers didn't approve of my bicycle cluttering up the aisle, nor the smell of my net, which reeked of a kipper's socks on washday. I kept my head low and thought of the fishing that lay ahead.

Two changes and three hours later, I arrived at the village station near to the lake. I said my farewells to the stuffy pinstripes aboard the cabin and alighted the train, cycling along the platform into the welcoming silence of deepest Wiltshire.

Jade looked magnificent upon my arrival. I cycled down the gravel track towards the dam to see an explosion of green in the woods, complemented by the milky turquoise waters. The sun was high and a gentle breeze was pushing towards the dam.

I stood and looked up at the lake. Somewhere, out there, were two gigantic fish, going about their lives as they had always done, oblivious of the gentle angling forays made for them and their kind. I breathed deeply, smelling and tasting the heady balsam scents in the summer air. Monster fish or not, it was good to be back.

It would be evening, no doubt, before Chris arrived. So I had all afternoon to explore the lake and try to find its hidden swims. I would venture along the eastern bank and hopefully locate the laurel thicket that concealed the secret swim.

I left my tackle beneath an enormous oak that dominated the south-eastern corner of the dam. I passed through a rickety wooden gate and entered the lost wood. This was the most overgrown, jungle-like part of the lake. Nettles stood shoulder high, hazel and hogweed towered even higher, obscuring my view.

At first glance it seemed impenetrable, but soon I found the tracks of other anglers who had burrowed through the undergrowth, creating a maze of tunnels. I scurried along, stooping to avoid the nettles and crawling beneath the boughs of fallen beech trees.

The tunnels led to an opening near to a large Holm Oak. This was the entrance to the grotto – an icy cave that dripped water from its fanglike stalactites – that marked the entrance to the most secret part of the lake. I descended into the darkness, feeling my way along the rough, cold walls, breathing the dank air and hoping that I wouldn't disturb any sleeping bats. Stone steps led downwards, then levelled by the water's edge. I caught a glimpse of the pool through trailing ivies before the tunnel returned to darkness and rose, quite abruptly through the damp earth, emerging as a foxhole amongst the roots of a vast yew tree.

The woodland before me was remarkably open. It was dark yet alluring, punctuated by rows of lofty pine trees, their trunks devoid of branches but supporting a canopy of evergreen needles sixty feet up. I had heard of this area, it was known as The Cathedral due to its vast, echoing presence.

The ground ahead was steep and rocky, but there was a noticeable path winding its way up the slope. I headed forward, climbing the scree that I hoped would lead to the laurels. As I reached the summit I saw what I was looking for: a solid thicket of laurel that, I guessed, sprawled right down to the lake's edge.

I circuited the laurels, looking for a way in, but there was no obvious entrance. I tried pushing the branches aside and forcing my way through, but they were growing too densely. It was an impossible task, an impenetrable barricade.

A Leap of Faith

"I saw your bike," said Chris, arriving behind me. He had the look of a rag and bone man who was having second thoughts about taking the bike as scrap metal. "I knew you were here somewhere."

"Yes, erm, I left my bike by the dam," I replied, trying to look inconspicuous.

"You found the laurel thicket then?"

"I think so."

"Think so? You know so. Bet you couldn't find a way in though."

"It's impossible."

"That's what it wants you to think. It's doesn't like strangers snooping around."

"I do look pretty strange."

"Nonsense. You're one of us. Now, Mrs Laurel, behave. We are of honest intent, and require access."

Chris then grasped a horizontal branch that grew alongside the laurels, swung his feet forward and lay down flat, sinking slowly into deep leaf litter. With his toes pointing forward, he lifted his weight and gently eased himself under the branches, sliding quickly out of sight like a swimmer heading down a water flume.

I followed Chris' lead, sliding beneath the laurel branches and into the depths of the shrub.

Inside, the laurel was a tangled mass of branches that intertwined and locked together like a bird's nest. They blurred overhead as I slid rapidly beneath them. I could see Chris, twenty feet below, grasping at branches to slow his inevitable fall towards the water.

Casting at Shadows

Chris and I landed safely at the base of the laurels. Composing ourselves after our free fall, we caught our breath while surveying the scene before us.

The swim was like a natural harbour: laurel bushes overhung the water on either side, resting their branches upon the drowned limbs of sunken beech trees. The whole area was no more than eight feet wide and fifteen feet long, shallow close in but with deep open water beyond it. Seeing such stupendous fish at such close range, and in such intimate confines, must have made them look impossibly big. The swim looked barely large enough for a monster carp to turn around in, let alone live in. And yet we were planning to do battle here with these formidable creatures.

We decided to wait until nightfall before we fished,

so we climbed back up the bank to fetch our tackle and to explore other likely spots around the lake.

We returned to the laurel swim at 10pm. Guided by candlelight, and with rather too much port inside us, made our slides down to the water's edge slow and precarious. But Chris and I were soon settled beside the lake. We opted to use just one rod, which I would fish with while Chris acted as ghillie. Chris had secret bait that he'd been trickling into this spot each night, which the fish appeared to like, so we would be using this too.

Chris and I waited for thirty minutes. We sat silently and without motion; speaking in hushed voices to allow the atmosphere to grow. We imagined the carp swimming up from the deeper water adjacent to nearby snags and looking for their supper.

In the blackened water before us, the fish would be searching, exploring, seeking out each morsel that Chris was about to provide for them.

With his left arm extended, he placed the secret bait – salted chickpeas from a tin – one at a time onto his open palm before flicking them into the water, six feet away.

There were now five free offerings in the water before us, awaiting a hookbait to join them.

"It is time," said Chris, as he handed me a chickpea for the hook. I pushed it down onto the point and, with no other weight on the line, gently swung the bait out into the night.

With my rod rested in a forked stick, I wound a cylinder of silver foil around the line next to the reel and sat back to await the action.

Within seconds, the silver foil shot up and rattled against the rod. I struck, but felt no resistance.

"Too soon," whispered Chris, as he handed me another chickpea.

I cast again and settled down, but my heart was pounding so loudly that I was sure the fish would hear it.

"At least we know they're here," remarked Chris.

He was right and, what's more, we could detect the subtlest of movements in the water, faint swirls and ripples bulging and breaking against the muddy bank.

The silver foil twitched, making a short, sharp, "pssst" like a snake about to tell us a secret. Chris and I froze. The line twitched again.

"Steady," said Chris, "remember last time."

I kept my hands away from the rod and awaited further signs of life.

The silver foil, which had been hanging in a loose cradle of line, gently and gradually lifted towards the rod. I reached for the rod and, with my other hand, held the line for further indications. There was a dull pulsing on the end, as if an invisible hand were stroking the line.

"I think there's a…"

"Strike!" shouted Chris.

I jerked the rod upwards and to my right. The line thumped against something solid and the water erupted at our feet. The rod bent double and line tore from my reel in an unstoppable blur. It was as much as I could do to prevent the rod being pulled from my grasp.

The fish bolted from the margins, ignoring the safety of the snags and instead heading for open water, far out into the lake. My reel continued to spin furiously, its ratchet sounding like a heron practicing for the lead role in Figaro.

I had never felt such terrifying, absolute and unstoppable power.

The fish ran deeply and steadily, pounding on the line with each kick of its tail. It was so different to the lightning dash of a wild carp, slower yet relentlessly unforgiving.

"How much line do you have on that reel?" shouted Chris, as the never-ceasing ratchet droned into the night.

"About a hundred yards."

"Then you'd better clamp down now else that fish will de-spool you."

I adjusted my footing to gain a better balance and then cupped the reel hard with my left hand, feeling the rod judder then thump down hard with my right. I heaved against the fish. Its power was softened by the bungee effect of ninety yards of line and the 9ft cane rod on which I was playing it, yet I couldn't gain much control over this opponent.

The fish continued to pound the rod, the line following it through the darkness as it swam from left to right and back again.

"It's tiring," said Chris, as he searched for the net, "but that's a really good fish, so be careful as you draw it back."

With both hands on the rod, I eased the fish back, a yard at a time, pumping and reeling as I went. The fish continued to kick, but with less power than before. Slowly, ever so slowly, the stretchy sensation in the line began to ease and I knew the fish was drawing close to the bank. The water in front of us swirled and boiled, sounding like a full water butt toppling and then gushing over in a storm.

"Easy, easy!" Chris' words were well timed; the fish lunged, making one last attempt for freedom. But it was too late. Chris scooped with the net, water erupted before us, sending spray in all directions and then – the line went slack.

"We've got it!"

Gasping for air and with my heart pounding, I heard Chris hoisting the net ashore. I knelt down beside the net and, with hands shaking, fumbled at the mesh and felt the smooth, cool body of an immense carp.

"Wait! Just a moment," said Chris, "whilst I light a candle; we need to see this fish!"

I heard Chris fumbling in his pockets, then the

rattling of a matchbox before a grating and a blinding spark that illuminated the laurels above us. The soft amber glow of the flame became whiter as it made contact with the candlewick, its luminosity radiating around us and highlighting the fish.

"It can't be."

"I don't believe it."

But it was true. This was an enormous fish. A splendid carp. Stout and brutish and with a disproportionately large tail. Its bronzed scales revealed the scars of previous encounters; its mouth gasped, opening and closing as it tried to make sense of its new environment.

"First time on the bank," said Chris.

"It would be rude to weight it, though," said I, "its presence, and nature of its capture, is one of legend."

But we did weigh it. And we did stare. And we barely believed.

"It was a noble warrior," replied Chris. "A monarch of the lake. And a capture to keep secret, for a very long time."

We lifted the carp from the net and back towards its natural environment. We said farewell, then slid it back into the water.

As we stood up and looked out into the blackness of the night, Chris said, "You do realise, your fish was the biggest carp caught this year?"

Suddenly the pursuit of monsters seemed very, very, real.

1998

XI

A FLICK OF THE TAIL

Jade Lake epitomised how the character of a carp lake is influenced by its surroundings. All those dense mature woodlands of oak, beech, ash, horse chestnut and plane trees intermingled with Scots pine, giant redwood, larch, alder, willow and yew. It had an infused atmosphere, of sprawling vegetation framing a canvas of shimmering jade-coloured water and deep blue sky. Painted by Nature, it was an earthly paradise with gifts above and below the water.

I'd fished Jade for five years, always enjoying just 'being there'. Plenty of carp were caught but, more importantly, the lake and I developed a mutual respect. I'd know when I arrived whether she'd had a good or bad day, just from the atmosphere in the air – whether she was tired and wanted to sleep or whether she was in a playful mood and would keep me on my toes. But Jade always whispered to me "I am bigger than you," so I fished humbly and politely, always remembering that I was her guest.

There is an expression, that when we are in the presence of Nature we are "Closer Thy God to Thee."

The beauty of the landscape, the sense of freedom and the romance of the moment combine to release one's inner poet or artist. And so the traditional anglers at Jade sought to fish harmoniously with the water and its landscape, always refining our dress, tackle and tactics to be as timeless and organic as possible. We knew that, compared to the rich and long history of the estate, we were merely passing through and should tiptoe as gently as possible. Indeed, through our desire for things never to change, we acted, subconsciously, as guardians of the lake's simple yet fragile appeal, knowing that we were keepers of her secrets. But then, much to our horror, word got out.

At an early point during the syndicate's administration, before the extent of the carp stocks were known, a modern strain of fast growing mirror carp had been stocked. Given the richness of Jade's larder, these fish grew very large. But, unlike their native housemates, were comparatively easy to catch. This attracted a handful of new members who joined for the fish rather than the beauty of the lake. Blinkered by their desire to catch big fish, they lacked our sense of respect for the surroundings. They were not there for the lake or its heart-warmingly wonderful wildlife and history; they were there for these new, lumpy, bloated fish. One of the 'plastic' carp was landed at a weight so large that it equalled the previous British record. But it was a blubbery creature with pale grey skin and a sagging belly that made us pity its existence. Jade suddenly became known not for her myths but for this freakish and notably out of shape fish.

News of the capture alerted the carp-hunter's grapevine with rumours of 'a new and vast Redmire', a water with so many fish that could break the record that it barely seemed feasible or real. But it was real. And it attracted a very different type of carp angler whose singular focus was to catch massive carp. Watching these anglers fish was like seeing teenage boys hanging around the girl with the largest breasts in the hope that they might get lucky with a lewd grope or short-lived conquest. The look of insincerity in their eyes, and the desperate acts they took to catch 'the target' (using four rods, with baits not cast out but *rowed* hundreds of yards from their swims in fibreglass dinghies), was a shock to the system for a young romantic like me to observe. Whilst angling is fundamentally predatory, this new style of fishing had something sinister about it. It was all about the *conquest*, brutal warfareish conquest, rather than the pleasure of the chase and beauty of the prize. There was no gentle courtship with the lake and its inhabitants, no joy in simply 'being' close to that which we love; just aggression and exploitation. Jade, the most beautiful, stately, ladylike and motherly water imaginable, was being raped of its innocence.

The syndicate's new 'ultra-modern' anglers (who, I'm sure, appreciated the lake in their own way) brought with them a rigid, one-method, static 'must catch' approach to their fishing where everything, including their surroundings and fellow anglers, had to adapt to accommodate their tactics. They arrived with bow saws, shovels, transistor radios and a curt vocabulary that implied they hated everything they saw or did. Swathes of vegetation were cleared and levelled to house their enormous bivouacs and multi-rod set ups. Our cherished Double Vision swim, where I had recently landed the fish of a lifetime, was flattened during their invasion; I covered my ears each time I heard the anglers yelling eyebrow-raising profanities at the fish each time they missed a bite.

A FLICK OF THE TAIL

It was, perhaps, the use of boats that most changed the atmosphere at Jade. Although I'd used one several years before, to bait up during the closed season, never would I have dreamed of using one to row out my baits. (Surely, part of an angler's skill is to be able to cast accurately and discretely?) And I definitely wouldn't have dreamed of fishing across or into someone else's swim. Whilst I could see the benefit of placing one's bait directly amongst the free offerings, it seemed crazy to be doing so just so that they could fish tight to the opposite bank. Wouldn't it have been easier to set up on the far side and drop a bait at one's feet? Nevertheless, these anglers would arrive with boats, which they would row far out into the lake, often to within jumping distance of the far bank, whereby they would push long plastic poles into the lakebed to mark their baited spots. Then they would tip a hundredweight of hard-boiled baits into the lake, making the same sound as a child pouring a bag of unlucky marbles down the toilet. Hearing the boats return, clunking and creaking through a dawn mist, was like preparing oneself for a visit from the skeletal boatman sent to escort you to the eternal afterlife. Yet this was the new 'norm' and my first exposure to a very different side of carp fishing. Whilst I acknowledged that my 'gently-gently' style of angling, with one rod and a centrepin reel, would never "trouble the scorer", as they put it, I was appalled by their obsession with using technology rather than watercraft to catch fish.

Their rods were capable of casting huge distances (even though they chose not to cast with them) far in excess of the twenty yard limit of my centrepin; their super-sensitive electric alarms could tell the angler if a fish had asked for directions to its breakfast; and their taut nylon bivouacs were filled with electrified gadgets such as a radio, fridge, television and light bulb; all requiring powering by petrol generators that would chuff and burp like a flatulent waiter.) But whilst the tackle and approach was very different to mine, it wasn't guilty of any crime; rather it was the angler's mindset that I couldn't fathom, as though all the 'boys and their toys' paraphernalia was there to bypass the romantic courtship between a lake and its visitors. (As I stared at the red lights glowing from their swims at night, I couldn't help but think that their fishing had degenerated into a desperate and unloving 'next in line' transaction with a finned lady of the night.) But Jade wasn't that sort of hostess. She didn't give up her treasures easily. The anglers' profanities became louder with each passing month, as the big fish refused to appear. The lake took on a dull and sullen look, like rain on the horizon; the air beneath the waterside trees, once sweet-smelling and warm, became dank and gloomy; and even the smaller carp, once so visible in their vast shoals, retreated like wartime evacuees.

I knew, as I tiptoed past the deafeningly 'industrial' generators chugging along outside the anglers' taught green shelters, that it was time for me to depart. Jade was no longer the same. Like an opera singer without her voice, she had lost the magic that had once made her so special. Knowing that the din and devastation from these new anglers would colour my memories of Jade, I conceded that my time there had come to an end.

Opting to leave a syndicate – especially one as exclusive as Jade – can be an agonising move. Often it's a decision of the head that the heart struggles to accept. Rational thought over emotion. This might be okay if you're a scientist but is difficult to bear if, like me, instinct and gut feeling lead you. There are friendships to consider, the sense of belonging and identity one gets from being part of something, and the risk of never again having access to such fabulous fishing and surroundings. One minute you're making plans for the coming season, then you're questioning the expense, the time, the travel, or simply asking yourself if you still enjoy being there as much as you did. Ultimately you question what is was, really, that drove your change of heart.

At Jade the reason was clear: it was the infiltration of insensitive anglers, brought about by the presence of huge carp, which changed everything. If there were only small carp there, then they wouldn't have shown the slightest bit of interest. Nor would they have needed such brutish tackle or heavy-handed tactics.

A FLICK OF THE TAIL

I wondered whether a lake full of 'lean, feral, scrawny, runt carp' (as they called them) would escape such attention? Perhaps the way for me to preserve the gentle, simple, innocent and heartfelt style of carp angling, that I'd practiced since reading BB's *Confessions of a Carp Fisher*, would be to find and fish in an overgrown, intimate and very pretty little lake that contained only wildies? It would be unlikely to appeal to the oar-wielding marauders, and – in wonderful contrast – might be exactly what other traditional carp anglers might seek. Sure, even the most died-in-the-tweed traditionalist would whoop for joy if he or she caught a big fish, but size wouldn't be the 'be all and end all' of their quest. They'd simply lie back in the long grass alongside their rod and reel, gaze out to a scarlet-tipped float and allow the contentment of countless generations of anglers to wash over them. How nice it would be to blend into one's surroundings and out of one's time, to feel the warmth of the sun on one's face (rather than the green, alien-like half-light of Planet Bivvy) and escape the swearing, brush cutting, boat clunking, watch-checking, overly competitive and desperately urgent multi-rod bombardment of modern angling? The timeless beauty of traditional carp angling, sensed through purity of intent and warmth of heart, would be there for our gentle embrace; enabled principally by the presence of small, shy, 'significantly insignificant' and richly golden wild carp.

Beauty sure is in the eye of the beholder, and one's emotions can certainly cloud one's judgement, but one's angling ideal is so often influenced by image. For me, I need 'aesthetic harmony' to achieve my longed-for sense of timelessness when angling. My tackle, luggage, clothing, camping equipment, even the lake around me, has to look 'olde-worlde' and be as organic as possible. But most important is the *mindset* of the angler. Too much urgency, lack of environmental appreciation and care, and knowingly compromising sporting or gentlemanly values to exploit the fish, acts like a foghorn that shatters the ambience of one's time by the water. Whereas if the mindset is right, the image will follow as the angler seeks to perfect his or her rare and cherished time by the water.)

I knew, deep down, that Jade was still beautiful and whatever damage was being done would ultimately be repaired by time and the green wand of Nature. I was aware that there were still some areas of bank left untouched where small carp were still catchable close in, but the spirit of the angling at Jade – brought to life by those fishing there – was dying. Many of the original, traditional, syndicate members had left, so I wasn't able to share my stories or discoveries with people who shared the same values as me. Indeed, due to the increasing ridicule I got for using a 'wooden' rod, I was faced with the prospect of having to go undercover – using modern tackle – just to fish there. It wasn't me and it wasn't right. But at Jade? The place that had stolen my heart? I felt like seeing my loved one in the arms of another man.

I mentioned my heartache to Richard Battersby one night as he and I sat beneath his umbrella, sheltering from rain while fishing together at Jade. He was similarly upset by recent developments and was also intending to leave the syndicate. We agreed that the character of Jade would eventually return, but the cost of waiting for it to happen would be too great for our sanity. It was time to move on, but to where?

Richard remarked that he had been quietly observing my angling at the lake ever since he learned of my epic bike ride. He said that, as I'd stuck to my principles, maintained my angling values and felt genuine pain in seeing Jade being robbed of its charms, I had deemed myself worthy of some privileged information. He then spoke in hushed tones, as if handing me the greatest of life's secrets, informing me of an idyllic wild carp water where the timeless magic of carp fishing still existed. The pool had been introduced to BB in the 1940s and, because of its intensely captivating atmosphere and long history, was the inspiration for several carp pools in his books.

At some point during Richard's story, I must have fallen asleep because what came next was so magical that it could only have been possible through a blurring of dreams and reality.

Other than BB, only ten friends were ever allowed to know of the pool's existence. Their group had fished there since the 1920s, catching wildies and recording their exploits in a fabled 'Hidden Book'. When one friend grew too old to visit, he would hand his secret to another, and so the legacy of 'the ten' would continue. It sounded amazing. Perfect. A manifestation of everything I had hoped for in a lake. But almost too good to be true.

Richard drew closer and, whispering softly, asked, "When would you like to visit?"

From that moment on, I'm not sure if I ever woke up…

1998

XII

ON HALLOWED GROUND

After much deliberation, I decided to leave the Jade syndicate. My resignation coincided with me receiving a letter from Richard inviting me to fish at his special pool. Grief soon changed to excitement as I opened the envelope. It contained a beautifully written letter from Richard, a hand-drawn map of the lake, some photographs and a quote from the Hidden Book. I marvelled at the images and waited patiently as my tension to fish there grew.

Richard and I had agreed to fish at his pool in mid-August, just two weeks after he had first mentioned it to me. Preparations were made and we were soon travelling together in his car to the venue. The journey from his home in Gloucestershire to the secret location in mid-Wales had taken two hours but, as noon approached, we knew that we would soon be at our destination. My heart was racing as we pulled into a farmyard and switched off the car's engine.

"We're here," said Richard, his eyes beaming at the prospect of visiting his favourite pool. "But before we exit the car, you must promise me that the path here must never be followed; it is for the Brethren only." He then reached for my hand, took it and began shaking it as he said, "Once we were nine, now we are ten; never shall our number be eleven." It was, apparently, another quote from the Hidden Book. "You are the tenth member, Fennel. You've passed the first initiation, simply by being 'our sort'. Soon you will delve deeper and discover *infinitely* more."

I solemnly promised that the water would remain secluded, away from invaders and wielders of carbon rods, that its true location would never be revealed and that any breadcrumbs left would lead only to hungry swans. I added that I would remain true to the spirit of angling and fish only for enjoyment, never for gain. Richard smiled and opened the car door.

Our drive had ended in a muddy farmyard, one of those semi-derelict sites that indicate a long lineage of farming. There were old rusty tractors and cars, ploughs and harrows dating back to before the war, all abandoned as if time were frozen. But the vegetation growing up between them reminded us of the passing of time. There were saplings growing up through engine blocks, brambles knotted through tines, and what looked to be a large pumpkin asleep in the driver's seat of an old Morris Minor. (Richard joked that it probably wouldn't have passed its driving test, as it couldn't see over the steering wheel.)

The landscape around the farmyard was typical

Welsh hill country: steep-sided mountains covered in grass, gorse, heather and bracken, with wooded valleys in between. The lower and flatter part of the slopes were grazed meadowland, but behind the farmyard they were heavily wooded, rising steeply towards a sheer cliff of slate, beyond which I could see no further.

Richard pointed to the corner of the farmyard, near to a corrugated iron barn. "Over there," he said, "near to those elders. Do you see the path?"

"Not really," I responded, "but if you lead, I'll follow."

Richard and I left the car and made our way towards the promised pathway. We'd decided that my first visit to the water should not be with rod in hand, but should instead be 'open handed' to ensure a mind free from angling intent. So we had left our tackle at home for this visit and instead took only a camera and binoculars.

We pushed through the elders and along the rear of the barn towards a lichen-crusted wooden gate. The gate was set into a shoulder-high dry stone wall. Behind the wall was a dense thicket of semi-mature oak, beech and ash. The air beside the trees was damp and cool, making it feel as if dusk were falling. No breeze or birdsong brought life to the trees, yet the scene was strangely inviting.

Passing through the gate, we continued along a muddy track that wound its way up through the wood. The ground sloped away steeply to our right and I could hear a tiny stream flowing at its base, tumbling over boulders then forming silent pools amongst the shadows.

Richard and I walked for about ten minutes, deeper and higher into the wood. The sound of the stream intensified as it crashed against rocks and made small waterfalls, its route growing ever closer to ours.

"There, up ahead!" said Richard, "We're nearly there."

I looked up and saw a steep slate cliff towering in front of us.

"I didn't think we would be rock climbing today?" I joked, "I hope there's a ladder."

"Wait and see," replied Richard.

We reached the wall of rock and looked up. It was fifty feet high, dark grey with the same foreboding presence as a scornful headmaster. The length of the cliff spanned as far as I could see in both directions, yet the path continued along the base of the rock, heading down and towards the stream. I figured that the water must be flowing from somewhere, so maybe there was a spring or a culvert up ahead?

"So, tell me," said Richard, "would you go around, up or down?"

"Definitely down," I replied, "towards the stream; it must be flowing from somewhere."

"What about *straight through*?" said Richard, with a mischievous look.

Before I could comprehend his comment, Richard

was moving hurriedly to the right, feeling his way along the stone. After thirty yards he disappeared behind an angular protrusion in the cliff. His head then reappeared. "Come on, are you going to follow or not?" he said. Sensing an imminent surprise, I followed his route along the base of the cliff and, passing the angle in the rock, saw a rectangular opening in the slate.

"The miners' entrance!" exclaimed Richard. "Technically it's called a Portal, but it was also a drainage adit for their excavations, at least until they dug deeper."

I was aware from BB's writings that the lake had once been a mine, albeit a small one, but I'd not imagined that any mining evidence would remain. Yet here in front of me was a tunnel through the rock, six feet high and five feet wide, supported on all sides by stout timber.

"We're going in," said Richard, "but, as it's your first time here, we'll not bother with lighting a lantern."

I put my trust in my guide and followed his lead into growing darkness of the tunnel. The air inside was cold and stale; the ground beneath us was puddled with water that had dripped from the ceiling or down the walls; each footfall splashed and echoed softly down the tunnel and we became aware of the rasping sound of our own breathing.

Feeling disoriented by the darkness, I decided to count my paces. I needed to understand just how far underground we were travelling. Twenty paces became thirty; fifty became sixty. I then became aware of a glow in the distance that intensified into dazzling light as we reached the end of the tunnel. The air suddenly became sweeter and warmer, I could hear birds singing, leaves rustling on a breeze and – what was that? – a heron squawking away in the distance?

"Welcome to the Folly," announced Richard. "There aren't many people who have stood here; the locals think the tunnel is just an abandoned mine, so only a privileged few know where it leads."

The scene before me was that of ancient woodland sheltered at the base of four imposing mountains. I could see out across the treetops to the mountains beyond, appreciating the natural valley they had created. It was if the vegetation had flooded a hollow, much like morning mist does before sunrise, concealing what lay within.

The valley itself was small – ten acres or less – and I could see from the scree slopes and angular rock faces scarring the landscape that mining was conducted here, long ago. It was as if a Celtic quarry had been abandoned and allowed to set seed, sprouting new seams of oak, beech, rowan and holly. This, as Richard told me, was exactly what had happened. He explained that the quarry was very old. It had begun life as a gently flowing stream at the base of the mountains. Then, at the time of the druids, metal ores were discovered and small-scale excavation began. In return for their intrusion into the underworld, the druids made human sacrifices at this location, awarding it a deep

spiritual significance. Mining continued on an ad-hoc basis until the seventeenth century, when commercial excavations began for silver and lead. But excavations were never on a large scale. The extent of the open cast mining was only four acres of the valley, extending to depths of fifty feet, although horizontal mines were also present. These adits, reputed to be over two miles long (one of which drained water to the nearby river) had long-since been lost through cave-ins and flooding.

"So what of the lake?" I asked.

Richard paused, then with a look of a man

remembering a lost relative, told me of the lake's history:

"The Folly was once a thriving mine, supporting a small local community; then disaster struck. It was 1748 when one of the tunnels collapsed, killing all but one of the mining men. As a remark of respect to the widows of the village, the locals decided to close the mine. Picks were gathered and barrows cast aside. Springs soon swelled up from the base of the mountains and flooded the excavation, eventually forming a lake that exited the valley through a fissure in the rock, becoming the stream that we saw earlier.

"On the anniversary of the accident, the miners' families met beside the lake for the last time. They said their farewells then retreated back through the tunnel, sealing it from the outside with timber and stone. The fate of the mine would have remained so if it were not for one man, Evan Jones, who, in 1867, learnt of mine and of his birthright. He had been told that the men who had once worked the mine were called Freeminers. It was they who held the rights to the mine in perpetuity. As a descendant of the sole survivor of the accident, Evan Jones had exclusive rights to the mine.

"With commercial intent, Evan decided he would pursue his family's fortunes by finding and reopening the mine. He followed the path of the stream, worked his way along the cliff and found the derelict tunnel, it's entrance concealed behind a hundred and twenty one years of vegetation. He hacked back the foliage cleared the rubble from the entrance. With a lantern held aloft, he made his way through the tunnel and into a clearing on the far side. His heart sank. He was not greeted with the sight of a mine or even a lake, but that of a seemingly Neolithic forest. Nature had consumed the entire valley, concealing the miners' roads and excavations beneath a towering mass of beech and oak. A century's leaf litter had created a spongy, peaty carpet over the previously exposed rock; ferns sprouted from crevices in trees and earth, ivies and mosses covered every shady surface. Evan's hopes were lost. This was not a mine ready to be reopened. Furthermore, he had betrayed the wishes of his family by accessing the hallowed grounds. His urge for money had blinkered him into making a hasty decision, one that could never be undone. He returned to the village as a shamed man. Thus the story of Evan Jones became linked to the history of the mine and as a stark reminder of the cruelty of fate.

"Our story took a fortunate turn in 1923 when Owin Jones, the great-great grandson of Evan Jones, decided to make a pilgrimage to the site of the mine. Owin did not intend to exploit the mine; he visited merely out of curiosity. As an angler, Owin was intrigued by stories of a lost lake. Owin retraced his great-great grandfathers footsteps up the wooded valley and to the cliff, rediscovered the entrance tunnel and forged his way through to the ancient woodland beyond. Unlike his ancestor, Owin did not find a disappointing wilderness.

Instead he found a place of idyllic natural beauty, a wildlife haven and place of serenity. He realised that visiting there was not a violation; it was a gift. The valley was a shrine to the lost, a tranquil legacy of the fallen. It welcomed him.

"Encouraged by what he saw, Owin descended into the dense woodland of the secret valley, searching for the lake. He found a narrow stone stairway and, following it down, caught his first glimpse of the pool – a narrow finger of dark water overhung with trees. It was 'as motionless and lifeless as a slab of slate'. He watched the water for several hours yet failed to see anything move beneath the surface of the water. Alas, there were no fish to be seen. This didn't worry Owin; he knew of another water nearby, a small stew pond near to an old church that held large quantities of small carp. He could catch these fish and bring them here, seeding the lake and bringing life to its waters.

"Over the course of three years, Owin stocked nearly a hundred carp into the miners' pool. Then, in July 1928 he made his first cast for them in their new home. He was rewarded with two brace of carp, noticing that all of them fought strongly, looked healthy and appeared content with their new environment. He also commented that their scales, which had previously been bright and golden, had darkened to an earthy-bronze colour. He named them 'the black carp of the black hills'."

"How do you know so much detail?" I enquired.

"From the Hidden Book," replied Richard. "One of our older members found it back in 1957, hidden in a miner's building on the far side of the pool. He'd been renovating the structure to provide shelter during his longer stays and discovered it in a rusty tin hidden in a wall cavity. In it was a well preserved notebook – the journal of Owin Jones and the first of the Brethren."

"The Brethren?" I asked.

Richard explained that Owin had invited others to fish with him at the pool, sending each of them a letter written in royal blue ink on ivory-coloured paper. Nine letters had been sent, each entitled 'An Invite to join the Freeminers' Brethren'. With Owin's company, this made a total of ten anglers privileged enough to fish at the pool. The letters were dated 1st September 1928. Amazingly, each of the letters survived to this day, having passed from one generation of members to the next. 'Only when a member chooses to hang up their rods for good, or departs this world, can a letter be transferred.'

Owin and the original members had kept a journal of their activities at the pool for the first twelve years, writing up the log at the end of each stay and returning the book to its safe place in the walls of the ruin. The final entry was dated 20th October 1938, a sensitive autumnal tome as if anticipating a time of loss. The Second World War started the following year and no further comments were made in the book.

Twenty years had passed before the journal was discovered and the members rekindled the log-keeping tradition. "We now have a small library of these books," said Richard, "but none is more special than the first, not with so much reference to the pool's history." However, the missing years between 1939 and 1957 were crucial to the pool's history, as this was when BB was rumoured to have visited (as an exceptional guest). The exact date is unknown and like so many great stories, it was never clear how much was fact and how much was fiction; but his writings during this time showed influences from the supposed visit. The current membership had chosen to name the pool 'BB's Folly' as a noble tribute, whilst providing a get-out-clause in case the rumours were untrue.

"Enough recollection," said Richard, "you need to see it for yourself."

Richard and I walked slowly along a path worn into the rock, descending from our vantage point into a thicket of shoulder-high bracken and then into a shrubby jungle of rhododendron and holly that marked the edge of the wood.

We pushed rhododendron branches aside to reveal a series of steps cut into the rock at our feet. The gradient of the slope increased dramatically from this point to an angle more suitable to abseiling than walking. Entering was like prising open the door to a forgotten cellar.

The stairs appeared ominous yet enticing. What gems lay hidden down there? What secrets shied away from human eyes?

The stone staircase descended for fifty feet before we exited onto spongy humus-rich ground. What had begun as a stairway among the tree canopy had fallen rapidly into the jungle below. Never could we see more than thirty feet ahead, such was the density of the forest.

Giant beech trees now towered overhead, their trunks four feet in diameter, gnarled and contorted with age, crusted with lichen and blanketed in moss; lime green leaves appeared luminescent against the bright sky above. The air beneath the trees was earthy, musky and humid; smelling like a freshly opened compost heap. It felt like we were passing though the yeasty sediment of time, to a place where history mingles with the present.

The floor of the wood was strewn with fallen trees and rotting branches; ostrich ferns and bracken unfurled amidst sapling rowan and birch that grew up through a dense sub-canopy of rhododendrons. Clearly this place was not 'managed' in the conventional way, where tidiness undoes wildness. Rather, the policy appeared to be 'if it falls, leave it', so there were centuries of fallen, decaying trees – around which the path weaved, mirroring the random but inevitable cycle of life.

Richard and I clambered over and under the fallen boughs, often crawling on our elbows and knees to get to the promised lake.

WILD CARP

Soon I became aware that we were near water, hearing a coot startle and dash from its resting place and smelling the unmistakable scent of a carp pool – an infusion of cucumber, rose and sage. Then, my first glimpse of water: sunlight glinting on a motionless pool, which looked like a sunken mirror in a pool of green.

Richard and I slid down the bank towards the pool, stopping at the base of an oak tree that overhung the water. Climbing its boughs, we pulled ourselves up from the woodland floor, above the rhododendrons, to get a clear view of the lake. I could see that we were at the top of the pool looking down towards a broader and apparently deeper expanse of water. From our position it was evident that the lake was perhaps four hundred yards long and only fifty yards across at its widest point. The long sinewy shape gave it a riverine look that enhanced its intimacy. But what really amazed me was how the surrounding woodland dominated the pool. The expansive canopy of oak, beech and ash overhung two thirds of the water – their branches inching out across the pool like fingertips stretching to reach a distant friend. Only a narrow slither at the centre of the pool was exposed to the sky and receiving direct sunlight; the rest was dappled with shade beneath the contorted branches of the trees. I sensed that eventually the trees would stretch too far and tumble into the water. But not just yet. For now they looked strong and protective.

Beneath the trees, a sprawling mass of rhododendrons, holly, willow, dog rose and clematis cascaded down to the water's edge, which was fringed with aquatic bistort, soft rush and sedge. The water itself looked ominous and dark, its murky brown-green opacity resembling a lily pad in winter. Yet it was bristling with life: the surface of the water twitched with insects and the meniscus seemed to pulse, like the eyelids of someone dreaming. Richard and I joked that the pool was like a sleeping Medusa, that the trees were its snake-like hair, and anything that fell into the water would turn to stone and remain there for all eternity.

We climbed back down the tree and continued our exploration of the pool. Richard informed me that once we were beside the water, the lake was accessible from virtually any point. A narrow ledge ran all round it, carved by the miners to access the mine. Our route soon led us to the path, which was five feet wide and relatively level. Richard remarked that the path was sufficiently adequate to lie down upon when fishing, although in some places it was necessary to lean against a tree for safety, so not to slide into the water. Thankfully, I could see no evidence of any cleared 'swims' or pruning of vegetation. Fishing here would be jungle-style angling, stalking fish at close quarters. Richard said that the margins of the pool were ten feet deep and that the best fish lay close in amongst the 'crows nests' of sunken branches, roots and boughs that lined the margins.

The deeper water, though clear of these snags, was forty feet deep and too dark for him to imagine anything living there.

Richard explained that beneath the water, the lakebed still followed the contours of the old mine, with the lakeside path becoming a circular 'road' that corkscrewed down to a central pit at the far end, from which three horizontal tunnels ran deep beneath the earth. This added a unique quirkiness to the pool where, when facing the water, it was possible for the fish to be swimming fifty yards behind the angler. This, apparently, led to inevitable outbursts of 'they're behind you' whenever sport was slow or fish could not be seen.

Not so this day. We noticed three carp appear from the depths beneath an overhanging willow, swimming nose-to-tail as if only one of them had the directions. Then a slightly bigger fish boiled beneath the branches before bow waving into open water.

Carp! A definite sighting of carp! They were unmistakably wildies, too. Long and slender, none bigger than five pounds or so, that had obviously flourished in the seclusion and protection of this hidden valley. The Black Carp of the Black Hills, that had been introduced ninety years earlier by someone who had unknowingly helped to preserve a near-lost strain of fish, had introduced themselves to me on this, my very first visit to the pool.

1998

XIII

A CLACKING OF KNOBS

Two months passed before Richard and I returned to the Folly. The dull autumn skies boded well for fishing, and the trees, flushed with amber and copper, provided a soft glow to the otherwise subdued landscape. Given the Folly's rich history, the scene before me looked like a sepia postcard sent through time.

The time of day was also different to my earlier visit. The sun had recently set and the pool was bathed in dusk-light, held in that frozen time between day and night. The wind had eased and mist was forming in hollows, producing a savoury ripeness that smelt like a basket of freshly cut mushrooms.

Our approach to the pool was different to our last visit, when we had delved deep into the wood. This time we opted to keep to a high path circling the outside of the valley. From this vantage point I could see glimpses of the pool below, noticing that its mood had changed since summer. The water now was darker and peatier, like stewed tea in a rusty pot. Richard and I jested that we ought to have brought tea strainers rather than landing nets, but we were confident that the fish would still be feeding. Richard had recently received a letter from one of the brethren fishing at the pool, who reported that the fish were in a 'gluttonous frenzy'. He'd averaged six carp per day from a variety of locations, all on broad beans. The message had ended with an abrupt "Get here quick!"

There were two other reasons for our visit: firstly, this year marked the 250th anniversary of the formation of the lake; secondly it was the 70th anniversary of the brethren's custodianship. It was to be a gathering of anglers, each paying their respect to the fallen and to celebrate the pool that had so marvellously flourished during its long life. It would be 'a gathering by the lake and then an outing to a local hostelry'. For me, it would be an introduction to the guardians of the pool and an opportunity to prove that there is far more to angling than catching fish. It was also an opportunity for a party.

"I think you're in for a surprise," remarked Richard. "Things might not be as different as you'd expect."

I'd asked Richard about the brethren before: who were they, would they warm to me, and would I be expected to wear a tie for my inaugural meeting? But he had remained frustratingly coy about the whole thing. As we walked along the high path, heading for the miners' cabin, I was more concerned about the condition of my muddy wellies and threadbare trousers than the prospect of fishing.

The path followed a natural course between the

wood to our left and scree slopes to our right, winding its way between large boulders and clumps of gorse. We reached the far end of the wood, where I noticed a grassy clearing. In it, set against a wall of rock, was the cabin. Partially overhung by beech trees, it was a single storey building with thick stone walls and a slate roof. Wood smoke rose from a brick chimney and three narrow windows were illuminated by the amber glow of oil lanterns. A wooden veranda ran the width of the cabin, its entrance marked by long row of fishing rods propped up against the guttering.

"As you can see," remarked Richard, "we've done a pretty good job of repairing the old thing."

Richard, it appeared, was master of the understated. This was a beautiful and sympathetically restored cottage, looking completely in place with its surroundings. It was most definitely *not* the ramshackle fisherman's hut I was expecting.

"A fishing lodge built from stone excavated from the mine," said Richard. "The timbers and window frames were brought up from the farm and the rest was acquired by the brethren; it's our place of refuge and reflection." There was a welcoming feel to this building. I imagined the sense of relief at being able to retreat here in a hailstorm, or relaxing in front of a fire on a long dark wintry night, or sinking into a warm bed rather than a damp sleeping bag. "Sometimes," said Richard, "we never even leave the cottage, such is the appeal of a good book, a lie-in, or the compelling banter between friends."

As if on cue, laughter erupted from within the cottage. Then an announcement: "They're here!"

Richard and I arrived at the cottage, placed our fishing tackle and luggage on the veranda, and approached the door. On it was a wooden plaque, into which were carved the words:

'Supreme Art is a traditional statement, passed on from age to age, modified by individual genius but never abandoned.'

"W.B. Yeats," said Richard, "it sets the tone for our fishing here, although the experience is usually more haphazard." He then pushed open the door and we were met by a blast of heat from inside and an almost deafening cheer from behind raised tankards.

The Freeminers' Brethren. I stood there stunned, suddenly realising why Richard had been so secretive about them.

"Okay," I said to Richard as we moved forward into the cottage, "so when were you going to tell me?"

"Actually," he replied, "I thought it would be more fun to show you."

We moved further into the room, being welcomed with hugs and enthusiastic handshakes from people I knew already. In fact, they were my eight closest friends, with whom I had fished for many years.

"But we only saw each other last month," I blurted, "couldn't you at least have 'tipped me the wink' or engaged me with a secret handshake?"

"Good point," exclaimed a voice from the corner of the room, "but your inauguration begins now; after all, your arrival coincides with that of Blue Vinney. Gentlemen, present your knobs."

The eldest of the Brethren approached me carrying a large tray held at waist height, on which was placed a small knife. "Young Master Fennel," he said, "we invite you to clack your knob with ours in the spirit of Thomas Hardy; please step forward to enter the circle of friends."

I hesitated, causing Richard to nudge me forward

into the centre of the room. This ritual promised to be a little too Masonic or even masochistic for my liking. I imagined Blue Vinney to be standing in the shadows with a video camera, getting his kicks, and that the size of the blade on the tray represented the anticipated size of my 'membership'.

"Gentlemen, reveal your bags," said the elder, "let us expose our cheese."

Before I had chance to react, each person revealed an assortment of paper bags marked with blue and red lettering. The elder then produced a large box and placed it on the tray.

"The first cut is yours, Fennel," he said, and then proceeded to open the box, showing its contents to be the largest block of cheese I had ever seen; comfortably fifteen pounds in weight, blue-veined and smelling like a pig farmer's wellies on a hot day.

I picked up the knife and pressed it into the hard crust of cheese, scouring out a crumbly wedge that I then placed into my hand. One of the paper bags was opened and presented to me on bended knee. Inside were spherical cobs of dried bread, each about the size of a golf ball. I glanced at the bag once more; on it were printed the words 'Moores Dorset Knob Biscuits'. I reached inside and took one.

"Clack Clack, clack, clack, clack!" chanted the group. What was I supposed to do? One of the members motioned that I should apply the knife to the biscuit, to break it open. This I did, hearing a satisfying crunching noise as I twisted the blade to prise it into two pieces. I applied the cheese to one half of the biscuit and put it in my mouth. The taste was heavenly: sharply, eye-wateringly, bitter and tangy at first, which quickly mellowed into a smooth, creamy, 'tongue on the teeth' way. It was like biting into an extra mature Stilton laced with battery acid.

"Wow! That's extraordinary, amazing, delicious…" My expression of delight caused another cheer and a loud applause.

"He passed the test," shouted one of the members. "Reckon he likes it," said another. "Our sort," said a third.

A free-for-all on the block of cheese ensued with numerous wedge-shaped knives appearing from pockets. Paper bags rustled as excited fingers fumbled for their next biscuit. A pewter tankard filled with dark frothy ale was thrust into my hand. Amidst the frenzied chatter and crunching of biscuits, I felt a hand on my shoulder and heard Richard's voice saying, "Welcome, my friend, welcome…" I turned to see him smiling at me. He then raised his other hand towards me. In it was an old crumpled envelope, on which was written, in royal blue ink, 'An invite to join the Freeminers' Brethren'.

1998

XIV

THE FREEMINERS' BRETHREN

The people I'd met in the miners' cottage were Mike, Darren, Peter, Mick, Dave, Pete, Bill and Roger, otherwise known as Prof, Rocket, Isaac, Demus, Phinehas, Magpie, Burton and Styx. Richard, who'd proposed me, was known as Angelus. All were friends whose nicknames captured the 'Dan Dare' style of boyish adventure and comic book humour for which the group is known. I'd been given the nickname 'Fennel' when I'd joined their group two years earlier. At first, I thought it was a nod towards my career as a gardener and that I'm a very gentle 'swaying in the breeze' kind of guy. "Nah," they'd replied, "it's because of that incident at Jade – when you boiled the herb with bucket of birdseed to make your uniquely flavoured bait, but then couldn't get the smell off your hands for a year." The name, like the pungent scent of aniseed, had stuck and I would be for evermore known as Fennel – he with the green and slightly pongy fingers.

Each person had proved themselves worthy for inclusion in the Brethren by being 'eccentrically authentic', at least in the eyes of modern society.

Phinehas was wearing authentic World War I trench officer's breeks, yet had peroxide blond spiky hair; Rocket had once turned a lake and all the trees around it pink when he set off a sky-diver's smoke bomb to mark the start of the fishing season; and Styx could brew beer so strong it could stone a donkey, yet he always seemed to be on his fifth pint. Mostly they believed passionately and genuinely in the traditional spirit of angling, as captured in the books by Izaak Walton, H.T. Sheringham, Arthur Ransome, BB, and Bernard Venables. Each was a humble countryman, attuned to the changing seasons and delicate needs of nature, and spent more time outdoors than cooped up indoors "breathing yesterday's trumps," as Prof would say. All were patient and sensitive fellows, enriched by the history of angling and compelled to fish simply and seasonally with vintage tackle in wild places. Most of all, they enjoyed their times together.

(Whilst the preservation of wild carp requires serious conservation effort, the friends knew never to take *themselves* seriously. "That duty," they would say, "is best reserved for people with something to prove. It's better to be the yeast-like catalyst stirring things up than a bloated piece of bread destined for the oven. Our role is to be the agent, not the crust.")

Anyway, back to the story...

"Hey, Fennel," said Styx, "we had you there for a

moment, you should have seen your face; you looked like you'd walked into an orgy without a flashlight!"

Styx was the last of the Thames Professionals, a boatman paid to guide clients to the best fishing spots on the river. He had proven himself worthy of membership by rekindling this tradition and pursing a vocation driven by purpose more than money. Most of us were privately envious of his lifestyle, frequently dreaming that we were sitting in his boat by the weir and not, as was often the case, on a chair in a sterile and claustrophobic office.

"The Blue Vinney cheese met with your approval then?" said Isaac. "It's Dorset best; used to be Thomas Hardy's favourite, eaten as you did with Dorset Knob biscuits." Isaac was the great raconteur of our circle, a man who genuinely valued friendship and would speak long into the night, reminiscing tales of old. His stately presence and meaningful delivery held our attention and made him our favourite storyteller. Naturally, he had been the elder statesman leading the ceremony.

"Did you know that Blue Vinney used to be illegal?" said Magpie. "The European Union decided that its production methods were far from acceptable." Magpie was the researcher of our group, equally at home in a library as at the lakeside. A consummate perfectionist, his knowledge of angling history and obscure fishing facts made him the chief archivist amongst us, although his extensive collection of historic tackle and books had earned him his feathery name.

"What do you mean by 'far from acceptable'?" I asked, half wishing I hadn't spoken.

"That rich salty flavour you tasted…"

"Yes."

"…is traditionally achieved by curing the cheese in horse manure."

Magpie paused, expecting me to wretch or look feint, but I remained calm and inquisitive.

"The cheese was outlawed, but we've found a Dorset farmer that sells it 'under the counter', though he no longer flavours it with dung."

"That's a relief," I said.

"Indeed; he now makes it by wrapping the cheese in really sweaty horse leathers." Magpie raised his eyebrows, "Which keeps the taste but eases the stench."

Heaven knows how the original cheese smelled; the current version brought more tears to my eyes than if I'd eaten a raw onion.

"It'll put hairs on your chest," said Demus as he sucked on his pipe. "It's the best cheese by far. And clacking open these Dorset knobs is a rite of passage for we brethren." Demus had a dry sense of humour and spoke the truth. A role model for many of us, he was the quintessential traditional angler, a reflective man who had a look of confidence and a rock 'n' roll credence that indicated that nothing really surprised him, though he'd act bemused to save us from appearing naive.

Also, he had the best beard in the angling world, a perfect King Edward that made our emulative attempts look like fluff on a weaver's jacket.

"That beard's good for ticklin' them Okey Birds," said Prof, in his soft Devon accent. Prof was a true West Country lad, born on a farm and raised to appreciate the country. Contentedly individual, he fished simply, using a lifetime of skill to catch his fish rather than 'selling out' to the false promises of modern tackle and automated tactics. "The bait MUST be on the hook," he would tell us, as he condemned the self-hooking rigs preferred by modern anglers. We understood. In his eyes, it was the clear 'hair' line between right and wrong. Prof was also the one who had fished at the Folly the longest and as such had an intimate knowledge of its mood and fish. He knew when to go fishing and when to retreat to the cabin for a cup of tea or to rest the swim. Because he was here now, I guessed that the fish had stopped feeding, or his urge for sweat-pickled cheese had overtaken his desire to catch.

"Need a top-up Fennel?" shouted Rocket, from across the room. "Hang on in there, I'll bring the jug before it corrodes from Styx's ale." Rocket was famed for his explosive celebrations on June 16th. But, like all of us, he enjoyed nothing more than a pint at a day's end, so long as it was drunk from a tankard or glass with a handle.

"Save yourselves for the pub," said Burton, reminding

us that this was just a taster and that the real drinking was to follow. Burton was used to such gatherings, often bringing a sense of irony to the proceedings. He'd once gone to a meeting of hard-nosed carp anglers that had gathered to discuss the latest developments in rig design. The conference, he claimed, was titled, "You'll feel a prick if you bend it like this." The only pre-requisite of entry was that every attendee had to bring an example of his or her latest end-tackle to discuss and debate its effectiveness. It was an 'I'll show you mine if you show me yours' event. Burton waited for his turn, patiently listening to the camouflaged masses exhibiting their latest "stiff ones, pop ups, dissolving socks, zig rigs, bent rigs, blow-backs and all manner of anti-eject do-the-fishing-for-you tomfoolery." When asked to show his 'killer rig' he stood up, reached inside his pocket, and brought out a manila envelope. In it was a size eight hook tied directly to twelve inches of nylon line. With an unfalteringly straight face he continued to talk through the process of side hooking a piece of sweetcorn and then, as the crescendo to his presentation, he explained how pinch a piece of bread flake onto the hook. The crowd looked on in disbelief as Burton paused, thanked them for being "a wonderful, *wonderful* audience" and asked whether they wished to see his encore, where he would explain how to use a catapult.

"Good observation," said Phinehas, "let us de-cheese and descend upon the tavern." Phinehas was the purist and deep-thinker of our group. A wearer of tweeds, breeks and fine waistcoats, he would usually be seen reading poetry or theology down by the lake, smoking 'herbal' cigarettes "to clear his mind" and generally enjoying a contemplative and relaxing existence. His approach to angling was uncompromising, challenging and cavalier; he represented absolute courage of conviction and took no quarter when defending his beliefs. It was his self-appointed duty to confront anyone who disturbed the peace and tranquillity of the waterside, be it canoeists, politicians or other anglers. His party piece was donning a vicar's dog collar and preaching to groups of lager-swilling anglers about the sins of consuming 'the evil drink', whilst himself swigging whisky from a bone china tea cup and saucer.

"Are you ready, guys?" said Angelus as he headed for the door. "It's time we paid our respects before journeying to the alehouse."

We donned our jackets and each took a lantern from a shelf near the door. Heading out of the cottage, we walked a well-trodden path down to the edge of the lake. The mist that was forming earlier had now thickened to a dense fog and made our line of lanterns appear like haloed stars.

Standing beside the lake, Isaac made a speech about the significance of this anniversary, of our gratitude to the pool and to the miners who had given their lives at this special place. He poured a libation of ale into the water and we swore that together we would continue to extol the traditions of angling and the virtues of a simple life, always to protect and praise wild carp, and never to compromise the serenity of the pool. We each lit a candle and placed it onto a bundle of dried reeds held by Isaac. He then stooped, lowered it to the water and gently pushed the raft so that it floated out into the lake. We watched it drift silently into the fog, knowing that the flames would eventually sink and fade, to lie for eternity with the miners at the bottom of the pool.

1999

XV

THE EMBOWERED

The Folly, in its secluded valley, was somewhere to escape the bustle of modern life while fishing for carp that had also avoided the passing of time. Great satisfaction could be found in escaping one's woes and finding one's dreams, being temporarily free from a life that would otherwise wrap itself around us and carry us along towards a more predictably boring fate.

For the first time in my life, I sensed that circumstances were taking me away from that which I loved, but not so at the Folly. Here I could still be free, being truthful to myself and living as innocently as I had done ten years earlier when my quest for wild carp had begun. I was keen to maintain continuity with that precious time, so that whenever I went fishing I could experience things as they'd always been. Whilst other areas in one's life might evolve and become unrecognisable, it's important to keep the child within alive. Being able to see the world and interpret ones emotions with childlike wonderment ensures we stop and look at a sunset or rainbow, walk barefoot across dewy grass, smile when we might otherwise cry, and know that we should stick up for the little ones who just want a quiet life in their little pond in a remote corner of nowhere. Wild carp, being the gold at the end of our rainbow, encourage us to think like that. They remind us that we don't have to be brutal, or heavy-handed. Fishing for them is more of a 'softly-softly' and 'ever so gently' activity; an 'after you, I insist' style of angling where nothing is urgent and everything is special. Just being part of their environment, moving slowly – not through stealth but because we're not in any rush to do anything – enables us to feel just as much part of their world as the deer and badgers in the wood, the waterfowl bobbing on the water, the ferns unfurling, or ivy climbing slowly up the trunks of the trees. Understanding this was crucial if we were to 'connect' with the rich atmosphere that's possible to savour when fishing for wild carp.

Of all the places to fish at the Folly, an area known as The Embowered was the most special. It was an intimate corner of the lake, a place where two huge beech trees leant out over the water and locked branches, creating a cloistered 'ceiling' with boughs resembling gothic arches of a private chapel. It was a still and shady spot, with moss covering the rocks and ferns growing from the crevices of each intertwined limb. A small spring wept from an exposed rock face and its water trickled gently into the pool beneath the overhanging branches.

The area was normally viewed from a high cliff above,

THE EMBOWERED

Angelus relaxing in The Embowered...

...while wildies relax just ten feet from him.

but with great care it was possible to climb down into the base of The Embowered to sense its overwhelming calm. Those who stood there agreed that The Embowered was the heart of the pool, the place from which all life sprang. It was the epicentre of the lake's spirit, a place to connect with the personality and living entity of the Folly, to most immediately sense its mood and likely playfulness of fish. The Embowered was also the most undisturbed area of the pool. The fish knew this, often using it as a spot in which to rest or feed. It was possible to inch oneself along the beech boughs, with slow but deliberate movements, to lie horizontally above the water. Here, one could look down and see these fabulous fish swim just an arm's length away, silhouetted against the slate shingles at the bottom of the pool and blurred by the reflections of leaves upon the water's surface.

The Embowered, in truth, was a place to forget about fishing. It was somewhere to contemplate and give thanks to our maker. Here, the fine line between air and water – the film between the known and the unknown – was blurred. It was like kneeling before an altar, not knowing whether to look up or look down. The words of Izaak Walton would inevitably drift into one's thoughts, saying, "God never did make a more calm, quiet, innocent recreation than angling." I am sure that he never made a more fitting place to angle for wild carp than at the Folly.

The fishing at BB's Folly was always relaxed, always

simple. The carp would patrol the margins in small shoals of up to six fish, which could be intercepted with a half-handful of bait thrown up to six feet from the bank. Mostly we'd fish with worms, maggots or pulses, almost always using a float fished lift style. At dusk, the fish would 'cloop' on the surface, feeding on sedges and moths. So we'd fish for them with small pieces of breadcrust. Typical of wildies, they had the ability to transform 'sleepy silence' into 'chaotic cacophony' when hooked, causing centrepins and anglers to scream as they rocketed away from the bank towards a sunken tree or sharp underwater cliff. Whilst we would always share stories at the end of the day, of fish seen, caught or lost, we never spoke of them outside of the Folly. Other anglers could only dream of them, through images that emerge at bedtime…

A Bedtime Story for Anglers

XVI

BEYOND MIDNIGHT

In daytime, when light, shadow and form depict the scene, all can be seen and comprehended. A mountain, a moor, a circle of trees surrounding a 'bottomless' pool; they are an all-too-quick assessment of beauty, nothing more than a snapshot of the obvious. At night, the world is different. It is a time when anything is possible.

It was midnight at the Folly. All was silent and calm. Slowly, as if waking from a deep sleep, the pool began to stir. Ferns unfurled their fronds and swayed gracefully, washed by invisible currents; ivies and honeysuckles drifted in mid-air as if floating upon a nocturnal tide; mushrooms pulsed in and out, breathing in the night air; ancient trees creaked then straightened their limbs. The scents of the earth, which had lain static amongst the leaf fall, whisked up and spiralled through the woods. The fabric of the pool had awoken. The spirit of the Folly was everywhere: in the trees, the soil and water. Everything was animated and alive, revelling in the quiet of night.

The air, which was thin and transparent, grew heavier and more humid. Dew began to settle on the leaves around the pool and a faint mist began to form. Then, as if pulled by the gravity of the Earth and the Moon, the sky began to buckle and the waters of the pool began to rise. The lake's surface shimmered and rippled, then a billion drops of water broke free and flew skywards, like rain in reverse. The water gushed upwards, gaining momentum, until the valley surrounding the pool was filled with dense spray. It was impossible to tell water from air, for they were one: a humid vapour, a blurring of elements; a merging of worlds, like molten mirrors colliding in the night.

Vortices formed at the centre of the crater that once was the pool. Something else was stirring. The wild carp of the Folly had woken from their slumber. The Black Carp of the Black Hills had swum forth.

A procession of carp emerged from the mist, each nose to tail as they ventured upward, swimming in a broad anticlockwise spiral. The fish swam higher into the vapour, breaking free from their usual constraints, free from the attentions of anglers and free to roam wherever they liked. At the front of the procession was the largest, oldest and most respected fish of all: a wild carp named Keiya. Her body writhed and her tail kicked, sending a ripple through the vapour that spread out across the valley. Trees swayed and bent. Rocks shirked and cowered; all made way for the monarch of the pool.

Keiya was the last survivor of the original fish

introduced to the pool. She had lived in its waters for nearly a century. The pool was hers to command and rule. In all her years, she had never been caught, though anglers desired her. They questioned how she could grow so large and yet evade capture for so long. Surely she must feed? Why did she not like their bait? But they did not know of nights like this, where the forest became the carps' playground and the woodland became a larder in which to forage.

Keiya and the procession of carp continued their journey, rising up to swim amongst the trees. Soon they were high above the treetops, circling above the Folly. Their tails kicked and thrashed as they began to swim faster and higher above the woods. The mighty shoal of fish swam with greater purpose, whipping up a breeze below. The breeze became a whirlwind – an updraft sucked into the vortex of carp swimming high above the pool. The leaves of the trees rustled, the ground rumbled in anticipation of a nocturnal crescendo. The wind became a gale that lashed at the trees and whipped the vapour into a piercing spray.

And then, nothing.

The valley became locked in a silent freeze-frame, as if time had stopped. The carp had spiralled into apparent nothingness, a mere blur, part of the vapour and essence of the pool.

Silence.

A glow from the east marked the coming of dawn.

The darkness of night, which had once been absolute, was losing its hold on the landscape. The scene began to lighten.

There! Poised as if frozen in a celestial sea, were hundreds of carp, motionless in the slate grey sky, a halo of fish floating above an empty pool. Water dripped from their fins, then from the trees; springs burst from the ground and a tumultuous downpour drenched the landscape like a wave crashing over a rock face. The trees shuddered and dried their leaves. Streams poured into the rapidly filling crater, bringing life back to the heart of the lake. The carp, looking down on this scene, sensed the rebirth of the pool. They writhed their bodies and kicked with their tails. One by one they broke free of their trance and fell swiftly into the reformed lake.

Crash! Kaboosh! Sploosh! The carp dived into the pool with purpose, keen to taste fresh waters and begin a new era. The vegetation resumed its usual forms and everything settled for another day of confinement. All, it seemed, was normal. But there was something different. The pool was incomplete. One carp hadn't returned to the water.

Keiya had been high in the sky when she became frozen. Her muscles had powered her higher than any other. She had watched the other fish wriggle free from their torpor and fall back into the pool. But she was trapped.

Poised high in the sky, with daylight breaking upon the horizon, Keiya felt vulnerable and alone. Isolated in a cold and windswept place, she yearned to return to the pool, to its warmth and safety. She struggled and writhed and shook her head. She broke free and began to fall. But she could see that the trees had returned to their contorted forms. The air about her felt dry. She began to feel feint. She was falling, falling faster than she had ever feared. The world around her became a blur; she saw the pool drawing closer and closer. But it was too late. Keiya felt her scales and fins turn to vapour and her body turn to mist. She landed without a splash, merely billowing out upon the surface of the pool.

Remember Keiya when you gaze upon a misty pool at dawn.

2002

XVII

THE LAKE AT THE EDGE OF THE WORLD

Waking from a long sleep can be as disorientating as not allowing oneself to sleep. I was aware that I'd slept, but couldn't remember for how long. For some reason, my brain wasn't functioning properly; in fact, it felt like a block of cheese left out in the mid-day sun. I rose slowly to view my surroundings. I was not alone. Isaac, Prof and Angelus were with me, all suffering from the consequences of 'the day and night before'. Aha! Now I remembered. We'd been at Angelus' stag do.

Being a country-type, Angelus had chosen the Dorset Agricultural Show as the venue for his stag party. We had marvelled at steam engines, farm machinery, livestock, rural craft displays and home cookery demonstrations. And then, at lunchtime, we'd discovered the beer tent. First we decided to 'sample' a few ales, just to get a taste. Then, as we staggered further down the tent, we discovered a local farmer selling some seriously nuclear-powered and equally ominously named cider called 'Diesel' and 'Suicider'. This stuff wasn't your usual amber-coloured, transparent and fizzy 'pop' sold in mainstream pubs; rather it was dark, still, and contained invisible ninjas that did their best to smack your face and pull your bottom lip behind your ears with each sip. For public safety, it was served in quarter-pint cups. So, naturally, each of us ordered four cups at a time.

I forget whether we stayed there for long, or whether anything at all happened for the rest of the day, as my next memory is of me staggering back to a campsite, alone, in the middle of the night. I knew that our crew were camping there, though I didn't have a tent of my own; rather I could vaguely remember that Prof had mentioned that he'd parked his Barbel Bus (a well-equipped camper van) at a local campsite. I'd not seen the bus before, but had somehow found one and decided that I'd sleep in its awning. If it wasn't his, then I'd apologise to its owners and move on to the next one. I must have found it, as I was now sitting in silence with my head in my hands, watching Prof – who was in a similarly fragile condition – standing poised as if in mid-stride, holding an empty kettle and, it would seem from the confused and weary expression on his face, trying to remember how to fill it with water.

The silence was broken when, in a fragile whisper, Angelus said, "Does anybody remember what we talked about last night?"

Heads remained firmly in hands, refusing to respond. Then, from beneath a pile of crumpled clothes in the footwell of the camper van, came the muffled words: "I do."

We turned slowly towards the unexpected voice. The clothes began to stir and rise. A head appeared like a hedgehog waking from a long, cheeky, hibernation in a laundry basket. It was Romper, a fellow friend with a legendary nose for a party and a nickname that had come from his insistence on wearing an adult-sized romper suit when fishing.

"Where did you come from?" exclaimed Isaac.

"Erm, I was with you all afternoon and evening," replied Romper. "In fact, I was the one who stopped Angelus and Fennel from riding piggyback into the exhibition ring to join the Argentinean Bareback Horse Riders."

"Lucky escape," mumbled Angelus, "though I remember none of it."

"Anyway, you lot, do you want to know what we discussed last night, or not?" Romper peeled a stale sock from his brow, rubbed his eyes, and rose to tell us more. "I remember that we talked about carp lakes, *wild* carp lakes, and the most *secret* ones at that."

"Fennel," said Romper, "do you remember how we concluded the conversation? Do you remember us talking about the Worcestershire pool?"

"No?" I replied.

"Here, take a look at this map; the one you were so keen to inspect last night." Romper then handed me

Prof's AA Roadmap.

"There," announced Romper, "on the border between Worcestershire and Shropshire, is Sheringham's Pool."

I stared at the map. Hazy memories returned of excited voices, shared secrets and stories of immense 'double figure' wild carp living in tranquil, untouched surroundings.

"That's not far from where you grew up, is it Fennel?" remarked Angelus, as if it was the first time he'd made the connection in the past 24 hours.

"I know," I replied, "but I can honestly say that I know nothing of this pool."

"Sheringham's was the one pool we tried to fish as kids, but never could," said Romper, sighing as he remembered the pool. "It's fourteen acres of the purest water, rich with weed and surrounded on all sides by mature trees. It exists in the middle of a very private thousand acre estate, is miles from the nearest road, and yet, because of this, is exactly the type of lake sought by wild carp hunters." Romper paused, then calmly said, "*Big* wildies were rumoured; tales of twenty-pound fish; alas, permission to fish was never granted; though I did hear of some guys from Manchester who poached it in the eighties; they caught lots of mid-sized wildies, and hooked bigger fish, but could never land the big ones."

"If there was ever a pool that we are destined to fish, then this is it," said Angelus.

"I know, said Romper, "you told us last night; alas,

the estate is heavily keepered, with no chance of viewing the lake without getting caught."

"Hmm," said I, "Does anyone have a clipboard? I feel a bird watching trip coming on."

Our group sat in Prof's camper van with a look of stunned amazement, as if we'd just found the Holy Grail in one of its cupboards. The map was passed from one to another, each producing the same gasps of wonder.

"I know that country," said Isaac, "the red clay is highly fertile soil, famed for producing big carp and very tasty potatoes; it runs from Herefordshire in the south up to Shropshire in the north; starting with Redmire Pool and ending with the Patshull carp lakes near Wolverhampton."

"Fourteen acres, you say?" enquired Angelus.

"And completely unfished," replied Romper.

"Fennel," the group declared, "it looks like you've won yourself an errand. Visit the pool and report back. Just don't get caught."

From the back of the camper, Prof looked up from his kettle and saw us ogling his map. "Eureka!" he exclaimed, "All I had to do was turn the tap on!"

The following week saw me scrambling through dense woodland as I made my way to the lake. I was cut by brambles, stung by nettles and caked in mud from a wrong footing by a stream. I'd been walking for nearly an hour, having left my car in a layby on the outskirts of the estate. I had my old bird watching book and sketchpad with me, hoping, as I'd taken my first steps beyond the 'Private Property, Keep Out!' sign, that the punishment of being caught as a grown-up ornithologist would be no harsher than when I was a child.

The terrain had risen gradually as I walked alongside the stream. This was good news, supporting my calculations that it would lead me to the outfall of Sheringham's Pool. But I was walking quickly (hence my earlier fall) as the sun was setting and I wanted to view the lake before darkness fell. I also had a personal mission to complete, sensing that I was near to completing my childhood quest to find the ultimate wild carp lake. I was also slightly annoyed that I hadn't already discovered this water, as it was only thirty miles from my childhood home. I'd prided myself in viewing every lake on my Victorian map, yet I wasn't aware of this reputed gem that had existed right under my nose. The reason, as I'd now discovered, was that my old map ended just one mile short of this location. To my young mind, the world beyond the map did not exist. It represented 'the mysterious unknown', and yet there was a lake there – at the edge of my childhood world – that was potentially so great as to be unimaginable.

"It can't be much further," I thought, as I trampled the thousandth bramble to the ground. The stream was flowing strongly and soon I heard the gushing of water over a sluice. I noticed the slopes of a dam and, as I clambered up its grassy bank, made a mental list the things I was hoping to see – and not see – in my perfect lake. There had been so many pools discovered, so much promise and failure. Could this pool be 'the one'? Romper's description of it was so evocative, yet it is so easy to succumb to the dream of 'lost' wild carp waters.

What I really craved was a tranquil and natural wilderness, somewhere to escape the growing pressures and stresses of life, especially the expectations of others for me to 'grow up' and get boringly serious about the financial and practical responsibilities of adulthood. I needed be free, to dream and gaze upwards, to look for faces in the clouds; or to peer down into watery depths to let my soul glide with the fishes; somewhere I could whoop for joy when the overwhelmingly beautiful delight of being truly alive took hold. For I am a man of nature, most at home in a natural environment. I do not 'conform' to the rules, styles and 'targets' of a world where we are expected to contort ourselves to fit in. Like the wild carp I sought, I was knowingly different, happily smaller and less bold than my cousins, and very much out of fashion with the trends of the age. If I could find somewhere quiet, out of the way from all that 'progress', I might be allowed to exist unchanged. How apt, therefore, that it is at exactly such 'forgotten' places that wild carp thrive. A creature that's most happy when it's left alone. I could relate to that, because I knew, deep down, that I was looking for a place as much as a fish. Somewhere, if the need arose, for me to visit for a long time. Perhaps for a whole Waterside Year...

I wasn't disappointed. Sheringham's Pool revealed itself to me with such grandeur that my preconceived images of the lake caused me to blush. They were like comparing a marigold to a passionflower.

The following is quoted directly from my angling journal, written while viewing the lake for the first time:

'I am standing on a dam looking out across a wild and unspoilt lake. I cannot speak; all I can do is stand, stare and dream. Its waters are reflecting the coppery autumn leaves of the beech trees above; I can hear kingfishers 'peeping' as they dart across the surface; and, upon the near-breathless air, I can smell the faint balsam of a distant poplar.

This lake is beautiful. Majestic. Serene. I feel pulled towards it, and it towards me, as though I am genuinely at one with the water. It has the most welcoming presence of any lake I have known. The best qualities of all my favourite pools, kneaded into one glorious vision. Like the winking of a flirtatious eye, it has the mystery of Jade, the intense atmosphere of the Folly and the intimacy of The Cottage Pool. If the entire lake lifted and swirled, revealing itself to be one massive wild carp, I'd be only mildly surprised. For it seems alive, breathing, enticing, beckoning.

There is a sense of fate in my being here. I have, after thirteen years of searching, found the most stunning carp lake I've ever seen.'

I knew that I would have to fish there, whether

wild carp were present or not. I could empathise with Romper's yearning for the pool and understood why it had become the height of conversation between impassioned (even if extremely drunk) anglers. The vastness and remoteness of the estate, the maturity of the surrounding woods, the clarity of the water, the trees that had fallen into the shallows to create a haven for fish, the extensive beds of reed mace and bulrush. And no signs of angling. There were no clearings amongst the lakeside trees, no level swims or – heaven forbid – builders' pallets dotted around the lake. It was entirely wild, and with huge potential. It had the presence of a giant fish in deep sleep, waiting to be woken. If we were to wake it, would it be playful or would it rattle our bones? We would have to find out.

2003

XVIII

THE SLEEPING GIANT

It's good having friends in high places; friends with a common goal, a shared purpose. Take Romper for example. He's a fine angler and an influential guy, having a 'glowing' curriculum vitae from his senior position at a nuclear establishment. A man to pull strings, open doors and sign leases. His phone rang. "Romper, it's Fennel, you were right, Sheringham's is amazing, I'm sending you some photos; you've just got to see this place…"

"Sounds great," replied Romper. "I'll put things in motion."

Ten months of correspondence, meetings and careful negotiations with the landowner followed. There was even a bottle of expensive whisky tabled as a 'sweetener'. Romper worked his magic, building trust and credibility until, in August the following year, he achieved a first in the history of Sheringham's Pool: an opportunity to form a syndicate to fish there on an exclusive basis. Clouds parted, sunshine shone from the heavens, and glasses were raised. Romper had done it.

I was fishing at the Folly when news of Romper's

success reached me. A message sent via the farmer's son said: "Stop fishing. Trial day at Sheringham's tomorrow. Four of us can fish. If all goes well, the lease begins next year." It was enough to make me jump into the lake with joy.

The following morning took forever to arrive. I spent the final night at the Folly, sitting in front of the fire in the miner's cottage, dreaming of all the adventures that might be possible at Sheringham's Pool. Eventually the lanterns inside the cottage became blackened with soot and yet the room remained light as the sun was starting to rise. I rose from my chair, packed my things and left the lake behind. If I didn't stop for breakfast, I could be at Sheringham's by 10am.

Four hours later, I was driving very slowly along a heavily rutted farm track that led to the pool. I was tempted to give a royal wave, knowing that I was one of a privileged few that had been granted access to the estate. We had the golden tickets, for the golden fish. I was floating on cloud nine. Shame my car wasn't.

The trouble with remote carp lakes is that they're accessed via remote lanes. Lack of traffic usually means that these tracks are pot-holed and obstructed by fallen trees, or by inquisitive wildlife that just won't budge. I'd already knocked branches, pheasants and a muntjac deer out of the way; I'd clanged the car on all manner of lumps and bumps and had grounded it temporarily when the track became deeply rutted. By the time

I'd reached the lake, I'd cracked the suspension, dented the front bumper, burst a radiator, and somehow lost an exhaust pipe and passenger window. But the damage to my car merely told me that I should have left the car by the road and walked the final mile-or-so to the lake. If I'd done this, all the urgency and tiredness of a long drive would have drifted away and I'd have slowed my pace to a natural rhythm by the time I arrived. Lesson noted for next time, if there would be one. Now it was all about making the first cast into a new water.

I was the first to arrive, so was able to stand on the dam (the only part of the lake that was accessible without a machete) and watch the water for signs of fish. Bubbles were rising in the left corner of the dam, and I watched them move slowly along parallel to the dam's wall as a fish rooted for its brunch. A breeze was pushing gently up the lake, towards a fallen ash tree on the fallen bank. This looked like a likely holding spot for carp, though the bistort weedbed on the nearside bank looked like it ought to be the lake's main larder, as it would undoubtedly hold plenty of snails and shrimp.

Eventually I heard the rumbling of a vehicle approaching. I looked away from the lake and to the track on my left, and saw an old Range Rover approaching. The owner of the estate, who was chauffeuring three of our group to the lake, was driving it. Romper was sitting in the back seat grinning like a schoolboy who'd just

eaten a whole pot of jam; his old friends Scarborough and Rapala accompanied him. This would be their first proper visit to the lake.

The Range Rover pulled to a halt, the anglers exited and removed their fishing tackle from the boot. I walked over to them.

"What happened to your car?" enquired Romper.

THE SLEEPING GIANT

"Don't ask," I replied.

The owner then wound down his car window and said, "Welcome to my pool; please treat it with respect, and let me know what you catch, as we have no idea what it contains. Sadly I can't stay with you as I have pressing engagements elsewhere." He then turned the car around and departed.

"Wow," said Scarborough, "this place is…"

"Amazing," we said in unison.

Seeing the pool in its summer splendour was even more impressive than on my previous visit. The beds of hornwort waterweed were thicker all across the pool and the scents in the air (a mixture of balsam from the poplars and pineapple from nearby conifers – apparently planted as game cover for pheasants) were much headier. The sky was overcast and the air humid, making the day feel more like late September than mid-August, and the 'dusky' light levels were excellent for fishing.

"Okay," said Romper, "here's the plan: we've got until 5pm to do some fishing – to find out if we like the lake and to see if we can discover what it contains."

"First objective is complete, the lake's lovely!" declared Rapala.

"Don't get your hopes up," advised Scarborough, "it might not contain wildies."

"Only one way to find out," said Romper, "the first one of us to catch makes history."

"Our main challenge," said I, "is that the only fishable places are along the dam, yet the fish-holding spots look like they're further up the lake."

"You're right," replied Rapala. "Four of us along the dam might be a bit tight; didn't anybody bring chest waders?"

"Actually," I replied, "I did, as I half-expected this situation. So, if you've no objection, I'll leave you here and see if I can reach the water's edge further up the lake; perhaps I'll be able to wade out beyond the overhanging trees to cast." They agreed, so I said my farewells and headed back to my car where I collected my tackle and walked towards the trees on the right bank.

The woodland on the right hand side of the lake was thinner than I expected – mostly mature balsam poplars, alder and oak – although an undergrowth of brambles, nettles, scrub birch, hazel and willow meant it wasn't easy to walk through. I found that by lifting my feet high as I walked, I could flatten a route through the nettles and brambles and slowly make my way towards the pool. Eventually I was close enough to the water to get a clear view of the lake. The weed, reeds and fallen branches made the margins a tangled mass of snags – unfishable unless cleared – though the water didn't look deep, perhaps just three to four feet off the end of the overhanging trees. But it certainly looked fishy. Everything about this area of lake screamed "Carp!" I was about two-thirds along its length where, judging by the increased thickness of hornwort weed, deeper water shelved up towards the shallows. And there, just on the drop-off was the fallen ash tree on the far bank. Not that far away – perhaps sixty yards – and most achievable to reach with a one ounce lead, but this wasn't my usual style of 'under the top tip' fishing. I reminded myself that, as this was a trial day, I would do what I needed to do to try and catch a fish. And, what's more, I would

be radical and fish with two rods – and electric bite alarms. Both lines would be hurled in cane-whimpering fashion to the snag on the far bank. My bait would be 'Smelly Brown' trout pellet paste, which had been wrapped in Clingfilm and left in the car during my trip to the Folly. It had hardened to a tough, barely kneadable, dough – ideal for staying on the hook during the long cast, perfect for withstanding the nibbles of small fish, and could be rolled into balls for catapulting free offerings into the lake.

    I donned my chest waders and, with rods in hand, waded out into the water until I had sludged and poked my way beyond the overhanging branches. With a wincing hurl I cast each bait to within six feet of the fallen ash and then, with the reel pickups open, drew the rods back to the bank where I placed them onto the Heron bite alarms. I rolled a cylinder of tin foil 'silver paper' around the line between butt ring and the next ring along, then climbed ashore. I laid down comfortably on my coat spread out on the ground, then awaited activity from any carp present within the pool.

Sheringham's had all the right qualities for wild carp atmosphere, and was old enough to house an old strain of carp. Estate records had revealed the lake to have been created in 1583, and the oak and beech trees around it certainly looked old enough to have been planted soon after. Some had trunks that were five feet in diameter. The maturity of these trees – and knowledge that the lake had not been fished (officially) in living memory – created a sense of 'hypnotic timelessness', as if centuries of dormant 'waiting' were culminating in this first day's angling, with layers of mystery unfolding with each passing hour. There was also a current in the air, a brooding intensity that, as I lay there, created a sense of respect for the lake. It was like taking tea with an ageing professor, someone who had forgotten more than I would ever learn, yet didn't need to prove anything. Soon, moorhens and coots were dabbing peacefully across the pool, oblivious of my presence. I drifted into a contented sleep, catching up on much-needed rest.

I woke, somewhat blearily, to a gust of wind rustling through the trees above. I guessed from the cramp in my back that I'd slept for an hour. I peered through the trees to the dam and could see my friends chatting to each other rather than sitting next to their rods. "It must be lunchtime," I thought.

Then, to my right, I noticed a trembling and flash of silver in the line of my right hand rod. The foil indicator had moved. I watched it closely. It twitched half an inch upwards then stopped. It then drew tight against the rod and remained there. No line was being pulled from the reel, or noise coming from my bite alarm, so I watched the rod tip for any further signs. Had a fish swum into the line? Had one picked up my bait and then dropped it? The rod tip juddered then relaxed. I moved over to the rod and pinched the line between my finger and thumb, drawing it steadily towards me. I felt a dull throbbing sensation, like holding a kite in a gentle breeze. There was something on the end! I lifted the rod and struck, half expecting to feel the jagging sensation of an eel.

Wallop! The rod lunged over and kicked hard. I was pulled to my feet and saw the line cutting through the water at speed, heading parallel to the far bank, round the bulrushes to my right, but thankfully away from the snag. I grabbed my landing net, jumped into the water, then marched out into the lake, stopping thirty feet from the bank and an inch short of the waders' limit. I secured my footing in the soft silt on the lake bed and then heaved against the fish. *Thump, thump,*

thump. This was no eel. Nor was it the usual fast run of a wildie. I wondered if the fish knew it was hooked? The slow, heavy fight continued. No fast runs, just a sullen weight on the line. I guessed that the fish must have been buried in weed, or that there was a huge clump of weed caught on the line. I shouted to the guys on the dam, but they didn't hear me. I pulled harder, feeling the near-dead weight of weed and fish lifting in the water and drawing slowly towards me. The water bulged in the middle of the lake as the fish made a kick for freedom. I caught a glimpse of golden scales smothered in weed. It was definitely a carp. "A good fish, could be a double," I thought as I applied more pressure. The rod began to creak beneath its cork handles and the line whistled in the breeze as I heaved the fish towards me.

Then, impasse. The weight on the line was too much for the rod to bear. Whilst I knew the line would hold, my rod was bent beyond the curve from which it would come back straight. Bamboo rods are lovely tools for playing smallish fish in open water, but not for hauling a big carp through dense beds of weed. I should have known better and brought my stepped up glass rods, or done what most anglers would have done these days and used a set of carbon thunder sticks, but I was 'connected' to my cane rods and one of them – at this very precious time – was connected to a very respectable carp.

Knowing that my rod could give no more without

fatally splintering, I decided to get closer to the fish. Already being at limit of my chest waders, I knew that I couldn't wade any deeper; but I could potentially wade further up the lake, into the shallows, and then back along the far bank to where the fish had become weeded. Obviously, this plan would require the lakebed to remain firm throughout; else I'd sink up to my neck or beyond. Was I prepared to drown for this fish? (Proudly eccentric, I'm always a rubber-footed step away from madness.) Actually, all that was going through my mind, as I began side-stepping through knee-deep silt, was whether any of the guys on the dam would start laughing as they saw a human-sized, tweed-wearing duck bobbing through the water. So I decided to do the chuckling for them, thinking of Herman Melville's words from Moby Dick: "I know not all that may be coming, but be it what it will, I'll go to it laughing."

Inching my way through the water, I felt swan mussels crunching beneath my feet and the silt become progressively softer and deeper. Then, a trickle of water into my waders. I had to stop, knowing that my plan wasn't going to work. The fish was still solid in weed, and I could feel it pulsing on the line, so I knew it hadn't shed the hook. Thinking through my options, I concluded that I would have to let the line go slack and see if the fish freed itself.

I lowered the rod and opened the bail arm of the reel. The tight ball of weed at the end of the line eased and

spread out, then the water erupted as the carp crashed on the surface.

"Farewell, carp," I thought. But then I noticed the line pulling across the surface of the water. I closed the bail arm and reeled quickly, tightening down to the fish. I felt the lead 'plink' through weed and then the rod kicked ferociously. I gripped the rod tightly and heaved against the carp. I couldn't afford for the fish to get weeded again, so I held the rod high with both hands and hauled upwards and away from the lakebed. The carp rose in the water, then swirled and thrashed on the surface. I kept pulling, pumping the fish towards me, eventually to within netting range. I pushed the net out as far as I could then sank it deep into the weed, holding its handle between my knees. Continuing to pull and not give any line, I drew the fish closer still and then, while holding the rod high in my right hand, plunged my left hand down into the water, grabbed the landing net handle, then pulled the net up quickly, scooping up a mass of weed and carp. The fish was in there, somewhere, though I couldn't see it for the weed.

By wriggling and twisting my feet, I was able to free them from the silt and then, bouncing along through the soft silt and weed, I ran like an astronaut on the moon to the bank. I threw my rod up onto dry ground and steadied the net and myself before grabbing hold of an overhanging branch and pulling myself out of the water. I composed myself, then laid the net on an unhooking mat and parted the mesh. I cleared away the folds of weed and saw – a carp! A fully scaled, bronze and gold treasure of a carp. Clearly outraged by being caught – probably for the first time – it flapped violently, doing its best to hit me with its massive tail. Yes, the tail was massive, and so was the fish. Not by king carp standards as it was very lean but, judging its size against the 36-inch arms of my net, it was 32 inches long. A thoroughbred powerhouse of a feral carp, and 'wildly' tempered, too. More importantly, the fish was our first from Sheringham's. I congratulated myself in catching it on my first cast and wondered whether it represented the average size of fish in the lake or whether, by freak chance, I'd caught one of the lake's biggest residents.

I removed the hook from its mouth and placed the carp in a sack, lowering it into the water so that it could rest there safely while I fetched the rest of the group to see it.

I stood up then ran as fast as I could towards the dam, my arms waving in the air and my voice shrieking erratically as I attempted to call to my friends. As I arrived on the dam, they heard my wailing and looked up from their sandwiches.

"I've caught one!" I shouted, "A carp! The lake contains carp!"

"Well done, Fennel," said Romper, proudly. "How big?"

"Definitely a double, I replied. "I've placed it in a sack so you can take photos."

"What, you want us to stop what we're doing," he said, "and take photos of a double-figure fish?"

"Yes!" I implored, "It's our first fish from the lake; you've got to see it."

"He's right," said Rapala, "we should take photos so that they can be shown to prospective members, should we secure a lease."

All of us then walked from the dam, along the path through the undergrowth beneath the trees, to where I'd been fishing.

"Is this where you caught it?" said Scarborough.

"Yes," I replied, "I hooked it over there, just off the fallen tree."

"No wonder we couldn't see you," said Rapala,

"we just figured you'd done your usual trick and gone straight to sleep."

"Erm, well, I did, though I managed to cast out first."

"So you caught a fish while sleeping, and we've been working hard at trying to catch one off the dam, but have yet to get a bite?"

"True on my part," I replied, "though I think you bitten through a few sandwiches in the past hour or so."

"Enough of this banter," said Romper, "let's see the fish."

I scrambled down to the water's edge and lifted the sack from the lake. The carp kicked, covering me in water. My friends gasped in awe.

"Strewth," said Rapala, "how big did you say it was?"

"Definitely a double," I replied, "though I've yet to weigh it."

I handed the sack to Romper as I clambered ashore, and then fetched the scales from my creel. We then carried the fish, scales and unhooking mat to a clearing on the edge of the wood. I unzipped the sack and, to the sound of air being exhaled through stunned mouths, lifted the fish for all to see.

"Erm, Fennel," said Scarborough, "that's some double."

"Yeah, now you mention it," I replied, "it does seem quite big."

Romper removed the weighing scales from their pouch, placed the empty sack on the hook, and zeroed them for weighing. He then removed the sack, laid it evenly on the mat for me to put the fish back in it, and then we lifted the fish onto the scales.

Staring at the dial in disbelief, Romper announced, "It's over twenty!"

"Comfortably so," said Scarborough, as he steadied the scales.

"Some double!" remarked Rapala.

"Guys," I said, "my best-ever wildie weighed twelve pounds. Are you telling me that this fish could be twice that size?"

"Yes," said Romper, "this fish is…massive!"

I posed with the carp while photos were taken, then we carefully made our way back to the water where we returned the carp to the pool. We stood for a moment in silence as we watched it swim away, then Romper said, "Do you know what this means? The very first fish from the lake was the biggest wildie any of us could have imagined. Indeed, it seems impossible that such a fish could exist. But if that's the average, then how big is the *biggest*?"

The revelation of what had happened, and the potential of Sheringham's to be the mecca for big feral carp, suddenly hit us. The rumours were true. This forgotten lake was the home of uncaught monsters.

"Romper," I said, "I think we'd better sign the lease."

2004

XIX

STEADY AS SHE GOES

The trial fishing at Sheringham's Pool continued for a year before we signed a lease. During this time we learnt that the average size of carp was about six pounds but bigger fish were present. There were perhaps one hundred carp in the pool, along with fish of other species, especially perch and eels. Whilst my fish remained the largest caught, there were half-a-dozen or so carp of this size seen swimming about in the lake – and two that were much larger. Clearly these larger fish were not 'extreme reversion' feral carp; rather they were long, lean common carp.

There's a blurred line when it comes to feral carp, with younger strains exhibiting the larger weight potential of their cultivated parents. Only the oldest strains, perhaps those with several hundred years of reversion, revert to the diminutive size and shape that's classically associated with wildies. This put us in a dilemma at Sheringham's. It contained a good head of small wildies, but also some larger carp. The small fish would be welcomed and treasured by wildie enthusiasts, whereas the bigger fish would attract specimen hunters that might disregard or disrespect the small carp while seeking another notch on their 'big carp' bedpost. I remembered Jade Lake, and its invasion of heavy-handed anglers, and felt a sense of dread at the prospect of Sheringham's suffering a similar fate. Its future was in our hands, though I wasn't entirely comfortable with such an obligation.

Being responsible for the most beautiful, precious, delicate and innocent thing, such as an untouched carp lake, is rather like being the parent of a young teenage girl. You know that, in her sweet way, she's grown up not knowing of her physical appeal to others; but all of a sudden, her assets are revealed and a string of suitors lines up at the door. Some have honest intentions, the majority do not.

Imagine the scene: you're at home, lying on the sofa and considering an afternoon nap, when the doorbell rings three times. *Three* times. "What's the urgency?" you think. You could jump up and rush to the door. Instead, you roll off the sofa, crawl along the living room floor to the window, then rise to take a sneak peek through a gap in the curtain. You spy a spotty, nervous-looking teenage boy standing on the doorstep. He's holding a bunch of flowers in one hand and adjusting a bulge in his trousers with the other. He's here for a date with your daughter. Your *daughter*. Your first-born angel and the embodiment of your every hope for the future. But she's growing up, taking bolder strides into the world, doing things on her terms and becoming her own person. You're her parent. It's your job to protect, educate and nurture her. You need to let go a little, while still ensuring she's safe, healthy and happy. Frogs will be kissed, some might even be toads, but there's someone out there who will love and care for her as much as you do. So you smile, leave the living room and go to answer the door. Burt Acneface might just be the one...

Establishing a syndicate is like this. Get the membership right and they will look after the fish, the place and each other, ultimately becoming a close and protective family; get it wrong and soon you will have a loved one crying on your shoulder. Fortunately for Sheringham's Pool, Romper and I had managed fisheries before. Our rule for prospective members was simple: those with red roses, strong aftershave, and a reputation for short-term relationships are out; those bearing wild flowers, an honest smile, and seeking long-term commitment are in. We decided that members would only be recruited from our close network of friends: those people we knew would appreciate the pool, liked enough to want to fish with them, and trusted sufficiently to keep a secret. Whilst personal recommendation might get someone onto a waiting list, actual membership required proven character. Our second decision concerned the vision for the pool: Sheringham's would not become

single-species 'big carp' water. Nature abhors monocultures, so the water would remain a mixed fishery. All the tench, bream, roach, perch, pike and eels had lived happily with the carp until now, so why play God and change their fate just because many of them compete with the carp for food? Whilst wildies were our favoured fish, members would undoubtedly enjoy fishing for other species at different times of year. We also opted not to stock the fishery with more carp. Genetic integrity of the strain of wildies was important, given that they were the real treasures of the pool, and although fishing for them wasn't easy (we averaged one fish per weekend) we decided that the catch rate was more to do with the carp not recognising our bait as food. Sooner or later the carp would 'switch on' and sport would become more prolific. Our third decision concerned the bankside management of the pool. It was so overgrown that fishing was virtually impossible without chest waders. Discrete swims would need to be cleared, with a balance of camping areas and stalking swims positioned around the lake. Cutting of vegetation would be minimal, always agreed with the landowner, and only done in winter so that the pruning would be less evident. Our approach would be to 'nurture nature' by sensitively felling and pruning trees whilst at the same time planting new ones to enhance the diversity of native vegetation around the pool. At no point would Sheringham's be allowed to look 'domesticated' with gravel walkways, wooden platforms or swims that could 'double' as helicopter landing pads. The very charm of the pool was its untrampled appearance and neglected character. Agreeing these principles upfront ensured the syndicate shared a common goal. There would be a sense of belonging amongst the anglers. As Scarborough put it, "We are a collective tribute to the traditions of angling and to a very special type of carp; not about glory hunting or exploitation, rather about sharing good times in our favourite place with our best friends. As custodians and conservationists of the pool and its wildlife, we are here to ensure its safe future."

I smiled, knowing that Sheringham's Pool was in good hands.

2007

XX

THE MONSTER OF THE DEEP

Three seasons passed at Sheringham's Pool. Years of contentment and careful nurture saw a strong relationship grow between the syndicate and the lake. Work parties created several discrete fishing spots around the pool, the carp became easier to catch, and specimens of other species were caught. Then came a shock discovery: Sheringham's held a monster carp.

The giant was first seen during the closed season while a member was scanning the shallows from a lookout tree. He reported that it was larger and different in appearance to any carp he'd seen in the pool. Broad, deep-bodied, and twice the size of anything we'd caught, it was a semi-scaled mirror carp that had somehow escaped our attention for years. So large was the carp that its observer described it as "a dolphin swimming amongst minnows." Perhaps this huge fish was the grand patriarch of the lake, the original stocked carp that had spawned generations of progressively leaner and more feral offspring? Or maybe, and more likely, it had been caught elsewhere and slipped into the pool by someone who didn't know the strain of fish in the pool?

Having a mirror carp in the lake proved to be concerning – that it might cross-breed with the wildies – and daunting, that if we were to hook it using our wildie gear, we might be massively outgunned by our opponent. We decided that the fish should be removed from the pool. Two seine nettings were undertaken, but no carp over six pounds were caught. Knowing the lake to contain much bigger fish, we concluded that the large carp had outsmarted us and evaded the net.

We fished on for another six months without seeing or hooking any of the bigger carp. The syndicate grapevine began to twitch and buzz about whether the monster existed and whether the bigger carp had disappeared. Had otters eaten them? Was someone stealing our fish? Had the carp taken a holiday back to the Danube? Or maybe, the biggest carp were setting us a challenge.

Hmph. A challenge, eh? Sure, we were still smart enough to catch them. Adrenaline pumped through our veins, eyes focused, lines were upgraded, stronger rods were purchased, secret baits were made and plans were hatched. The atmosphere at the pool intensified, like the hushed silence before an electrical storm. The game was about to begin.

Goggins, a member from Manchester, was the first to hook 'the beast'. He'd been fishing at night when one of his indicators sounded and his reel span into life. The fish had charged far out into the lake before he had chance to pick up his rod. The rod had thumped heavily,

THE MONSTER OF THE DEEP

its tip dragged down to the water as the fish made a lunge for freedom. And then the line parted. Goggins had to retreat to his tent for the remainder of the night, reliving the ordeal over and over until his nerves settled.

The ordeal happened twice more. Romper and a member called Rollo each fought the fish to within yards of the bank before the hook pulled free. They'd seen the enormous carp roll upon the surface. Rollo even had it thrashing over the drawstring of his landing net. But it was not to be. The leviathan escaped and returned to the realms of myth, albeit as a legitimate monster. How big? Romper and Rollo, who had both caught big carp before, independently said, "Could be a forty."

My encounter with the beast came on a drizzly autumn day, towards the end of a special Waterside Year spent at the lake. I was alone, fishing from a grassy area behind a dense bed of bulrush. Two baits had been cast fifteen yards out to an area of water beyond the reeds that I'd fed with hempseed, trout pellets and maize. I was nearing the end of an eventful day that had seen me bank a brace of double-figure wildies and a 'sleeveful' of snotty bream. Sport had since slowed; the pool looked lifeless and sullen, the sense of expectancy I'd enjoyed at the start of the trip had gone. My thoughts had turned to how I would pack away my tent without ruining its sodden canvas.

I reeled in the first of my lines and dismantled the

rod, wiping water droplets from its handle and cane. I turned from the water to place the rod into my holdall then heard a sudden 'shhhuup' of silver foil and then the chirring of my reel handle on the other rod. I span round to see the rod juddering in its rest as line ripped from the reel.

I threw my dismantled rod to the ground and lunged towards the rod in the rest. The line was tight and cutting through the water beyond the reeds. I grabbed the handle, clamped down on the reel and lifted the rod. The power of the fish was phenomenal, as though I'd lassoed a stampeding horse. It immediately jarred the reel handle from my grasp so I let it spin as the fish continued to charge out into deeper, clearer, water. The MKIV carp rod was bent to its limit as it strained against the might of the fish, which swam slowly and determinedly, sending sullen thumps through the line as it bulldozed its way through weed.

I felt my heartbeat quicken as I realised that I was locked in battle with something larger and more powerful than anything I'd hooked before. A sense of dread filled my veins as I realised that this was probably the carp that had evaded the net so many times before. It was most likely the 'uncatchable monster' that, for each second it was attached to my line, would inevitably haunt my dreams for a year.

Emotional trauma would have to wait. There was a battle in full, brutal, axe swing. I composed myself

THE MONSTER OF THE DEEP

and focused on the movements of the fish. A weedbed bulged sixty yards out, sending a patch of bubbles to the surface that fizzed like an erupting Polaris Missile. The fish's initial run slowed, so I cupped my hands around the spool of the reel and lifted the rod higher. Dull sensations surged through the line, most unlike the lightning-fast wildies or feral commons I was used to catching. The slow, ponderous, almost leisurely yet tormenting power; sudden kicks and then dead immovable weight. I knew that the fish was tiring, but I lacked the tackle or strength to control it. Pulling against the fish was like trying to row a steamboat with matchstick oars.

A patch of muddy detritus plumed to the surface above where the fish was circling. I kept a tight line as the fish thumped about on the bottom of the pool. Its runs were no more than five yards at a time, each attempt at freedom halted by another decaying weedbed. Soon, the weight on the line became constant as the fish became parcelled in weed and barely able to move. Was it lost, or was this an opportunity? Maybe the weed could tire the fish for me, doing the job that my hopelessly inadequate rod was unable to do? If I could maintain pressure, perhaps I could coax the 'dead weight' towards me? I reeled down gently until the rod was locked at the full extent of its curve, then steadily walked backwards pulling the fish towards the bank. I then walked forward, reeling as I did, and repeated the action until the large ball of weed was swirling and pulsating in a patch of mud and weed before me.

And then I realised the reality of my situation: that this fish, which was almost within reach of the net, could be mine. Others had *failed*, yet I was *winning*. I could be its first captor, the one to make history. I could land and cradle the fish, gloat at my success and await the praise and adulation of my friends as I shared news of its 'unbelievable' capture. *My* capture. My skilful and awe-inspiring feat of angling genius where I had landed a never-before-caught monster carp. My cortège of followers would hail me as "The King of Sheringham's Pool." My moment had come, the fish would be *mine*.

Oh how the treachery of desire destroys the innocence of angling.

The carp on my line knew nothing of its reputation. It was just a wild creature that had survived long enough for it to grow to become the largest fish in the pool. It would have preferred to have continued its day uninterrupted, feasting on hempseed, pellets and maize, to build its energy reserves before winter; but it had become tethered to some sort of annoyance that had deprived it of a good meal. I was hardly a superhero angler; my bait and the fish just happened to be in the same place at the same time. The weed had tired it more than me, so I couldn't even claim any skill in playing it. And besides, why was I getting so excited about catching a fish that was so far from my angling ideal? I'd spent eighteen years cultivating a belief that 'small and old is better than big and bold', so why all the chest-beating machismo just because I'd accidentally hooked an oversized carp?

I felt my heart sink as I realised that the real tug of war was not between the fish and me, rather it was *within* me: that the monster of the deep was not the fish; it was an ego-driven yearning that lies within, waiting to pounce forth from the darkness. I wanted to land this fish, yet feared the consequences of doing so and not doing so. Its presence threatened the existence of the wild carp I loved and the angling ideals associated with fishing for them. If I did land it, would my conscience allow me to return it to the water? I couldn't return it to my wild carp lake, and I would not allow myself to kill it. If I did, I would be the monster. The long feral carp — even though they weren't classic 'wildies' — were

too valuable. Could I move the big carp to another lake, as had apparently been done before? Perhaps, though I would have to be absolutely sure the water did not contain wildies, else I'd be guilty of ruining the genetic integrity of the lake's 'native' stock.

I continued to coax the fish towards me until it was swirling about four feet from the bank. The water became a cloudy soup of silt, leaves, twigs and weed. I caught glimpses of a huge tail. Then, a grey-cream flank and a flash of large golden scales. All incomprehensibly big. Images of Jade Lake's monsters came bounding into my consciousness, forced as though a gun was pressed to my head. My breath froze, a prayer floated to the heavens, and my eyelids narrowed as I moved forward to net the fish.

I reached to the ground with my left hand and picked up my landing net. I pushed it out into the water towards the fish. I pulled the rod with my other arm and felt the fish lifting in the water. Its head appeared on the surface; first I saw its mouth gasping and then I caught a glimpse of its eye – the key moment of connection – and sensed a look of anger and confidence that made me gasp. The carp rolled violently on the surface, sending a loud 'kaboosh' that echoed round the lake and soaking me with water. The rod kicked, jarring my shoulder, then…nothing. So sensation. No feeling. No connection. Just emptiness, silence and disbelief. I placed my hand over my eyes, clenched my teeth, and fell to my knees in despair. The fish was gone.

I opened my eyes to see a world blurred by tears. There was my line and hook, tangled in the bushes behind me; there was my reflection in the water, my contorted face reminding me of my anguish; and there was the net, robbed of its one and only task. I had come so close to landing that fish – the biggest carp I am ever likely to catch – but was it really the fish of a lifetime? My lifetime had been spent searching for wildies in remote or overlooked pools, not pursuing uncaught monsters. I am not a specimen angler seeking progressively bigger fish; I am a pleasure angler satisfied by all the subtle and gentle nuances, events and wildlife that enrich one's time at the waterside. So why was I

WILD CARP

crying at my apparent failure? Maybe it was because I felt robbed, that I would have felt the same if the fish were a wildie? No. An average wild carp would have been ten times smaller than the monster I'd just lost, thus my grief would have been ten times less. There was something about this fish's extreme size and sheer 'unbelievableness' – that I could have landed it with such antique tackle – that would have made front-page news. Perhaps that desire for fame and adulation pushed me to want to catch it? Again, no. The truth is that I felt, in that intense moment of loss, a completely useless, weak, inferior and pathetic example of a man, who'd had his chance and blown it. Like a boxer lying dazed on the canvas of the ring, I'd been outwitted, outfought and outdone by a stronger and better opponent.

I wanted to cast again for the fish, driven by the inevitable torment of unfinished business, but I knew I wouldn't. As I stood gazing out across the water, my hands placed on my head and my mouth blowing air as though it were releasing steam from a pressure cooker, I remembered Hemingway's words, "Man is not made for defeat. A man can be destroyed but not defeated." I certainly felt destroyed by that fish, but prioritising it over my quest for wild carp? That would be the defeat I couldn't accept. As George Eliot wrote, "The only failure a man ought to fear is failure of cleaving to the purpose he sees to be best." My purpose was to find an ancient strain of carp, living in a forgotten pool somewhere, and fish for it using traditional tackle. Maybe I could even play a role in preserving those fish and making others aware of their plight? This was my calling, my true purpose; I was not Captain Ahab about to exert obsessive revenge upon the brute from the deeps. So I brushed the mud and debris from my tweed jacket, straightened my flat cap, held my head high and proudly walked away, along a path that wasn't signposted by numbers. I knew that bigger wasn't best. A kingfisher is more agile and beautiful than a farm-bred turkey, and a daisy is more natural and unassuming than a towering sunflower, yet both are a fraction of the size. Such is the way of nature, where beauty is condensed as it becomes smaller. The fleeting glimpse, the treasure found in long grass; they're there but for the want of looking. My way forward, therefore, would be 'elsewhere', towards the heart of nature where I would listen for the twilight silence, then place my hand upon the ground to sense the pulse of life that sustains me. Going backwards to go forward, I would stay true to the dreams of my fifteen-year-old self.

2008

XXI

ACROSS THE MOORS

"The real voyage of discovery consists not in seeking new landscapes but in having new eyes."
Marcel Proust

I have visited hundreds of waters looking for ancient strains of carp. I've found some lovely pools and bigger, more dream-filled lakes, but all were inhabited by relatively young strains of carp; that is, ones stocked in the past three hundred years. These were beautiful fish, but now I wanted to discover the seemingly impossible – a strain of carp untouched since early medieval times.

It was a letter from Mike Winter that set me on this track. Mike had fished and searched for wild carp for over fifty years, holding true to the romance that they 'might' have been stocked during Roman or Norman times. His way of finding them was simple: follow the Roman roads to those locations where king carp are least prevalent and where human habitation is lowest. "The more remote or inaccessible the water," he said, "the greater the likelihood that this ancient strain of carp will have survived."

I set to work, scouring libraries for maps of Roman roads and overlaying them with Ordnance Survey maps to identify likely looking areas. Three areas sprang forward: The West Country of Devonshire and Cornwall, Wales, and North Yorkshire. I knew that Mike had already explored the West Country waters and identified the wildie hotspots. Unfortunately, nearly all of them had either been restocked with modern strains of carp, or were inaccessible to anglers. Yorkshire was too far from my Midlands home. And so I turned to Wales, home of my earliest angling adventures with a fly rod. But this time, I wouldn't be searching for wild trout, rather wild carp.

My initial research revealed that there were, or had been, wildies in the Black Mountains and even as far north as Anglesey. The area around Tintern Abbey, on the English borders, was also rumoured to be a hotspot. But it was the area around Builth Wells that really drew my attention. There were three Roman forts nearby – Castell Collen to the north, Beulah to the west and Brecon Gaer to the south. The main town has Norman origins and there is a Cistercian Abbey just a few miles to the west. A search of historic maps showed a series of Norman fishponds just west of the town and several mountain lakes further to the south. Could any of these hold wild carp?

Llyngwyn, a mountain lake to the north of Builth and run by Rhyader Angling Association, was reputed to contain wildies stocked in the 12th century by Cistercian monks from the nearby Abbey-Cwm-Hir. Although it was possible to fish this water, it was also a trout fishery, and I knew from experience that coarse and game anglers rarely mix well on the same water. So I delayed visiting Llyngwyn, preferring to find something wilder and more 'forgotten'.

I continued the search, identifying likely lakes on the map and spending my weekends visiting them one by one, but without success. This didn't mean they were devoid of wildies, just that I didn't see any carp when I visited.

And then rumours of a hidden mountain lake began to reverberate through the local angling grapevine. I'd been ear-wigging some locals at the Royal Welsh country show who, after talking about sea trout runs and the welcome increase in the local grayling population, casually started talking about wild carp and a landowner who was granting access to his previously out-of-bounds mountain lake. The water, they said, was "Dangerously close to the military zone operated by the SAS." It was heavily weeded and very shallow, but that wild carp had been seen there. They compared it to Llyngwyn, saying that this was the secret water near the old Roman encampment, "That only us locals should know about." "Let them tourists stay at 'gwyn and have their fun," they said. Finally, after mentioning the name of the lake, they agreed that the person to catch the first fish would be owed a bottle of ale from the others.

Perhaps I should get there first. But where was 'there'?

The military zone south of Builth Wells stretches for approximately fifteen miles in diameter and appears, somewhat ominously, as a blank area on the Ordnance Survey map. It's definitely one of those places best avoided or where, if you do happen to stray nearby, you make sure you've got a white flag easily to hand. That's not saying, however, that searching for wild carp is worth risking being shot by a stray bullet. I figured that the landowner offering this fishing must have weighed up the dangers before making his lake available, so I decided to find this tantalising water.

I couldn't see the lake on my maps, and although I found a few likely looking 'shadows' on aerial photos of the area, I couldn't be precisely sure where the lake was located. So I decided to do it the old fashioned way and ask local farmers if they could direct me. Big mistake…

I had four different sets of instructions from farmers who, I now believe, deliberately sent me in the wrong direction. Suspiciously, their directions also took me straight towards their neighbour's farmyard. I bet they were on the phone to each other saying, "Hey Dai, he's on his way, check out his hat Boyo; thinks he's Indiana Jones or something. Blummin' Englishman…"

The last farmer gave me directions that should have seen me lost forever. He had me driving up steep embankments, across rutted fields and then down a narrow dead-end track that was banked on either side by high hedges and ended in a gateway obstructed by a pile of manure. Unfortunately, the track was so narrow that I couldn't open my car door to get out. I couldn't turn around either, so I would have to reverse three miles back to the farmer who would probably be standing there with his farmer chums laughing their socks off.

I was about to begin reversing when an elderly couple came walking towards the gate. They were proper old-school ramblers with knee-high socks, stout leather walking boots, khaki shorts and rucksacks large enough to double as impromptu tents. They had seen my predicament and were on their way to help.

Winding down the window, I called to them with a rather pathetic-sounding, "Help, I'm lost." They came over and I explained that I was an angler searching for a shallow, weedy lake, hidden at the top of a mountain. To my delight the gentleman said that he'd passed the lake earlier that morning and that I would be able to reach it before lunchtime (it was 11am). He advised that I should leave my car at the bottom of the mountain and trek to the top, as the track was heavily rutted and the lake would appear more spectacularly if I'd had a proper climb getting there. He continued to say that I should steer clear of the red flags, as they indicated that live ammunition was in use.

The man showed me the position of the lake on his

map. It was located about six miles away, on the other side of a wooded valley and way up in the mountains that were surrounded on all sides by moorland. I said thanks to the couple and started the car's engine. It would be tricky reversing all the way down this narrow track, but the thought of seeing the farmer again and having the opportunity for him to (as they say in America) 'taste fender' encouraged me to floor the accelerator pedal and snarl as I approached his farmyard.

The sound of a car with its horns blaring while travelling in reverse at 50 miles per hour through a remote Welsh farmstead must have been enough to scare the ticks off a sheepdog. But it was worth it. The farmer and his neighbours had wasted my time and I was now on an urgent mission to, ironically, discover carp that had happily stayed put for centuries.

ACROSS THE MOORS

They weren't going anywhere, yet I felt as though I might have just missed them.

I felt somewhat duped by the time I parked my car at the base of the mountain. I'd received the run-around by these farmers all morning and was now looking up at a bleak and windswept peak, its slopes below swathed in coarse yellow sedge, too tough even for sheep to eat. This was Nature's country and no place for a romantic angler in a floppy hat and sandals. All around me, as far as my eyes could see, were mountain ranges and undulating moors. It was barren, exposed and harsh. And yet this was summertime. I couldn't image how bleak it must be in winter. It reminded me that Nature, in her untamed state, is savage and unrelenting. "Truly a wild beast", I thought, "not unlike the fish I'm pursuing."

2008

XXII

THE SANCTUARY

The mountain ranges around Builth Wells include the Black Mountains, Brecon Beacons and Cambrian Mountains. Together they form a triangle around an area of exposed moorland that is dissected by wooded valleys and tumbling slate-bedded streams. I could see all of this as I climbed higher in search of the ultimate wild carp lake.

I became aware that the oppressively bleak landscape around me was framed by its own context of mountain, sky and earth. I realised that it wasn't so much barren as 'isolated'. We get so used to the gregarious nature of our towns and villages that we forget how crowded our existence has become. Here, on this mountain, with nothing but a so-called 'wild' landscape before me, I realised just how much we have influenced our surroundings and tamed the raw beauty of nature. The sight before me, barren of trees due to centuries of grazing by sheep, was 'constrained' by us but still wild and inhospitable. If I were to find an ancient strain of carp, it would be here.

It took me over an hour to reach the summit.

Once there, I saw a lake set between a rocky outcrop and a gorse-covered peak. Virtually round in shape, and about eight acres in size, it was sheltered from the elements in an amphitheatre of green. Sheep, which were dotted around the lake but had been absent from the rest of the mountain, knew that this was a warmer, life-giving place. A buzzard glided effortlessly above the pool and a heron stood motionless on the gravel shingle of the lake's edge. The water was weedy, very weedy. It was covered in green leaves for all but a small area in the middle, which I guessed must either be deeper water or the source of a cold spring. And the lake, sheltered from the wind, was unrippled. It gave the water a harmonious, almost sleeping, look.

This was it: the water I'd been seeking. It was the lake that the local anglers had described, but more importantly I knew, from pure angling instinct, that there would be carp here. It just felt right. Normally, lakes in this area would only contain brown trout, minnows or perch. But this lake was super-rich and shallow: fertile and warm enough for carp to spawn and survive. "Perhaps," I thought, "there must be a limestone seam nearby that provides nutrients for so much weed to grow? Or maybe some mystical force is at work?" The scene, after such a long climb, reminded me of Shangri-La in James Hilton's *Lost Horizon*.

I paused and evaluated the facts: here was a lake near the site of an old Roman encampment, set high up in the mountains overlooking a miles upon miles of barren moorland. It was sheltered and secluded, rich and warm watered. All the elements were coming together. I just had to get down there and prove, finally, that carp were present.

Moving carefully towards the pool, I reached its shores without disturbing any wildlife. A slow, observant, walk round the lake's edges revealed that it was about four feet deep and that the weed – which was made up of a mixture of bistort and arrowhead – was incredibly dense. There were exposed shingle beaches all round, presumably because the water level was much lower than in winter. The water itself was gin clear. The margins were alive with minnows and the bankside sedges and soft rush were in flower. Gorse and buttercups were also blooming, making the scene feel more like May than late August.

Of course, I'd brought my fishing tackle with me. So I tackled up and opted to fish on the southern shore next to the rocky outcrop. This area was in full sun and had a greater amount of fry than elsewhere. I figured that if the water was warmest here, and the small fish liked it, then the carp would be nearby. I scattered small pieces of breadcrust into the margins and onto the weed and sat back to await signs of feeding fish. I hadn't seen any carp-like movements or activity as I'd walked round, so even though instinct was telling me that this was going to be 'the water', the inevitable self-doubt began

THE SANCTUARY

to creep in. Nearly twenty years of searching, hundreds of waters and endless strains of feral carp. It had been a long quest. Yet here was I within casting distance of my dream.

Out of the corner of my eye I saw a slight lifting of the weed, and then heard a faint and gentle sucking, similar to the sound of a kiss. I lifted the peak of my cap and stared at the water again. The weed was twitching and shifting as a fish worked its way from one piece of floating crust to the next. Another fish joined, then another. Very soon there were about a dozen fish feeding all along the water's edge. I needed to get closer to the fish, to get proof that they were carp. I couldn't bear the thought that I'd come all this way only to discover some gummy-lipped trout with a taste for bread.

I moved slowly and quietly down the bank towards the closest movements in the water. There, just twelve feet from me, was the confirmation I sought: a set of white lips, about the size of a fifty pence piece, rising up out of the weed. Then came a glimpse of a head and the characteristic flash of golden scales. These were definitely carp. But were they wildies?

I watched the fish for fifteen minutes, transfixed by how wild creatures, following their instincts to feed on pieces of floating bread, fed exactly the same as their more domesticated relatives. These fish probably had never seen bait before, yet they were readily taking the free offerings.

With my heart in my mouth, my head dizzy from adrenaline and my lungs breathing irregularly, I made my move to catch a fish. I attached a small piece of breadcrust to a size eight hook and cast it, without any other weight on the line, to one of the twitching weedbeds. Then, as the exact position of the fish became known, I drew the crust into its path.

The take came quickly. I never saw the fish, merely a sucking from beneath the crust and the slithering of line across the surface. I struck and the line drew taught as the fish bolted, ploughing through the weed. With weed and water bulging and swaying, I hauled the fish back towards me and into my net. The whole exhilarating experience, nineteen years in the making, lasted for no more than twenty seconds. I really did feel like a wild carp virgin.

After hoisting the fish ashore and parting the net's mesh, I saw the classic streamlined shape of a wild carp. About three pounds in weight, dark bronze across its back and with golden scales along its flank, it appeared to me to look much like a penny that had lain at the bottom of a wishing well for nearly twenty years. And then the moment of truth: was there a notch at the back of its head? There was, but barely enough to notice. What startled me, though, was its slender head and deeply forked tail, which appeared more like that of a dace than a carp. It was long, lean and solid: a very old strain of carp and my first wildie from this magical lake.

If Llyngwyn was the much-revered temple of wild carp fishing in the UK, then the place I'd discovered must be The Sanctuary. The fish had escaped the attention of anglers until now, so I swore to keep them secret until such time as others had stumbled upon them as well. I caught several more wildies that afternoon, none larger than the first, but I did disturb a fish in the margins that could easily have been five pounds. But size or quantity of fish wasn't the point. This was about completing the journey I'd started as a schoolboy. It was the culmination of so many years of reading, travelling and dreaming of wild carp. And yet, after just a few hours, I decided to leave. I could have carried on, catching and learning more of the lake's secrets, but that could wait for another day. The Sanctuary was a haven for the fish. And, as I soon discovered, for me as well.

2008

XXIII

GINGER BEER AND ALL THINGS HOLY

Imagine being stripped of all your possessions and social standing, then being transported to your dream lake to muse upon the things in life that bring you the greatest pleasure. Which of your most treasured things would spring instantly to mind? Would your list contain material objects, like a favourite rod or reel? Would the lake before you be on the list? Or would you prioritise intangible things, such as happy memories or the love of your family? Now imagine being thrust into a freezing, hailstone-pelted thunderstorm. How quickly would a warm, waterproof coat appear on your list of necessities? These were my thoughts as I returned to The Sanctuary.

My first visit to The Sanctuary was in August. Although the mountainside was subjected to blustery winds, the area of the lake had remained calm and I enjoyed an idyllic summer afternoon, fishing in shirtsleeves and throwing bread to the carp. But now, two months later, the leaden October sky was decidedly autumnal and the air was carrying a northern chill. The weather forecast predicted a big southerly front coming in for the weekend. "Perfect," I thought,

WILD CARP

"blustery conditions to stir up the lake and get the carp feeding."

I could see the weather front building in the clouds as I drove towards the Welsh mountains. It was dark and ominous-looking, curving the entire length of the southern horizon. I escaped its wrath until I reached Eardisland, when the rain began to fall. By the time I reached Builth, my car's wiper blades were flinging from side to side like a pair of deranged metronomes.

Arriving at the base of the mountain, I parked my car and gazed through the windscreen at sheet lightning flashing in purple-black clouds above. Somewhere up there, near the epicentre of the maelstrom, was The Sanctuary, its waters whipped into a furious spray by the might of nature. I gripped the steering wheel and cringed at my predicament. Should I attempt the climb the mountain in these lethal conditions, or should I sit tight and hope that the storm would blow itself out?

After twenty minutes of deliberating, and seeing that the rain wasn't easing, I decided to venture up the mountain. I climbed into the back of the car and pulled down the rear seats to access my waxed trench coat and wellington boots. Putting on my wellies and buttoning up the coat was like readying myself for battle with an aqueous army. I unlatched the door and pushed it open, hard against the wind that was trying to keep me contained. Rain lashed my face, stinging my eyes and skin. Trees overhead swayed and creaked, their branches cracking free and falling all around me. It was virtually impossible to stand upright against the might of the gale; yet, as the storm howled, I grabbed my rod and tackle bag and, with my head faced down to escape the blinding force of the elements, I leant into the wind and began my climb.

Conditions, as I ascended the mountain, were extreme yet spectacular. I was battered by wind and rain, pelted by hailstones and shocked into a cowering ball by the booms of thunder. The clouds overhead were so low they looked like I could reach out and touch them.

As I scrambled forward, up the steepest part of the mountain, the rocks became colder beneath my hands and my feet slipped amongst the scree and hailstones. My eyes were stinging from the wind, my cheeks were numb and my lips felt bruised. I looked up. I had only another six hundred yards to go; yet the clouds above had developed an ominous swirling pattern as if they were being sucked towards an infinite destiny. Lightning flashed all around, breaking the darkness within the cloud; the skies rumbled and crashed with tempestuous rage.

The eye of the storm was nearby, so I made for the shelter of a ledge beneath an overhanging cliff. Pushing myself against the rock, I was able to escape the worst of the wind. I could wait there until the squall subsided. I crouched down, hugged my knees and hid my face in my lap, preparing for the worst. Then the wind subsided and the rain ceased. I'd been expecting all manner of atrocity, like cows falling from the sky or a little wooden shack flying overhead, but none of this happened. I looked up to see a circular expanse of blue sky in the middle of the cloud and, right in its centre, a skylark flying high in the air and singing its little heart out.

"Get down you stupid thing," I thought as I stared at the bird, "it's not over yet." Sadly, my thoughts were too late for this little fellow. It was flung from the air by the returning gales and pounding rain.

The storm continued its assault upon the mountain and moors, but was moving away into the distance, easing as it went. I sheltered against the cliff, content to settle my nerves rather than test my endurance. Crouching on the ledge, I watched the storm move gradually into the distance and lighter clouds appearing behind it. It was like saying 'good riddance' to a bully at the end of the school year.

What was it about this place that made me risk everything, climb fourteen hundred feet into the oblivion of what must surely be the worst storm to hit these parts in years? Maybe, that the things we place greatest value upon are prioritised by their context in our lives. Just a few moments earlier, the lee of the mountain was a welcome gift, a place of shelter. Yet once I was there, I began to view the wider horizon. I thought of all the other things that mean so much to an angler, like time to fish; the quality and beauty of the waters we know; the fish themselves; the dip of a float or tug on the line. All these things are essential elements of our sport; one upon one building our values, beliefs so that, when combined, we identify ourselves as an angler. It's courage that swells from within, born of waters drunk deeply.

I remembered my childhood: there was nothing nicer on a hot sunny day than to be given a bottle of ice cold ginger beer – that feisty, zesty stuff you used to get that would bring tears to your eyes and make you sneeze. How things have changed. Ginger beer these days is mostly the sort of chemical-infused broth that pins children to the ceiling. I doubt it would create the same sense of euphoria that it did before. (Thank heavens for Fentimans, which still packs the punch of nose-twitching ginger fieriness.) But a grown man with the responsibilities of a wife, home and job requires something more than a sugary drink to cure his ills. He needs a greater distraction to help keep his life balanced. Something all consuming, like angling, which preserves his sanity and refuels his soul. The catalyst for such a release? Optimism and the promise of something good, fun and simple; just like the anticipation I felt as a child when my mother would bring a tray of chilled ginger beer out into the garden. And now, as a grown man, just like the promise of fishing for the secret carp of The Sanctuary. That's why I battled through the

GINGER BEER AND ALL THINGS HOLY

weather – to connect with The Promise.

"All things holy" is how I refer to the super-fine things that, either individually or collectively, give us greatest pleasure. They are our precious things. Simple things. A currency of sentiments. I looked at my weather-beaten creel sitting beside me. It, along with its contents, was drenched and looked ready to collapse. Yet I brought it with me for a reason. There were more effective – and waterproof – bags and rucksacks I could have used, but I opted for the item that brought me greatest pleasure: a silly old impractical creel that's older than me but looks great and warms my soul. I chose the company of

this creel, and in doing so demonstrated my belief that 'choice is the mortar that binds together the things and activities that make us who we are'.

The rain ceased, so I collected my things together, patted the walls of the overhanging cliffs in thanks for protecting me, and then climbed up a rocky crevasse towards the lake. It was good to be standing above the outcrop once more and looking out onto the moors. The wind had dropped and the marshy ground around me was steaming, as if the rain had triggered the heat of this once active volcano. I was surrounded by pillars of spiralling mist, each moving slowly down the mountain to diffuse amongst swathes of heather.

The sun broke from behind the cloud and, as I walked over the peak of the mountain, I saw the pool glittering like a million diamonds cupped in palms of green. I gazed longingly at the lake. We had been apart for too long. Too many months, too much stress, and no time to dream. Finally I was back in my elemental paradise, feeling most alive.

2009

XXIV

FREEDOM AND FORGIVENESS

"Man's life is but vain; for 'tis subject to pain,
And sorrow, and short as a bubble;
'Tis a hodge-podge of business, and money, and care,
And care, and money, and trouble."

Izaak Walton

I have a request, if you don't mind. I'd like you to put aside this book, pick up the 'phone and ring your employer, asking if you could work some extra hours this weekend. For free.

Did you do it? I bet not. And rightly so. In fact I can guess what your response was. But if you had made the call, would your manager have agreed to your request, or would you have been advised to stick to your contracted hours and not give up your precious free time?

Most of us, at some point or other, get sucked into the lifeless vacuum of work; the cogs of the corporate machine that we keep turning until one day, when we depart this Earth, we may earn the word 'lubricant' on our headstone. We question whether the effort is worth it, but the ever-increasing weight of bills and responsibilities that enmeshes our lives keeps us locked into the system and away from the people, things and activities we love. We become the pulse that keeps the beast alive, but the cost is our own lives. The natural world around us shrinks, crushed beneath the suffocating might of work. We hear a scream within, recognising the voice as our fifteen-year-old self. It's pleading with us to keep our innermost dreams alive. We pause and question how such soul-destroying yet 'obligatory' activities can drag us away from that which most defines us? We know in our hearts that our life has greater meaning, and that we should stop the treadmill, unplug from the system, escape to somewhere quiet, and enjoy being free. To an angler, this means going fishing. Which, to me, means fishing for wild carp at The Sanctuary.

Friday had arrived and I'd been instructed to work through another weekend. There was a deadline to be met and attendance was mandatory. No overtime pay, no 'thank you' card, just a deep and booming voice from above saying, "You will obey!" It had been the same for the previous three weeks. Extra productivity was demanded, with management beating the drum at an increasing pace. I'd already worked too many hours and was feeling the strain. Enough was enough. I needed to grab a fishing rod and get back to doing what I most loved.

There comes a time when you just have to say, "No!"

– to the requests and to the system. You can escape completely, seeking an alternative life, or you can play the game and go absent without leave. How you do it is up to you.

A short note to my boss, complaining of a sudden illness, saw me escape the paralysis of a weekend spent working and win back two days of living. The sense of freedom was overwhelming. I 'unplugged' from all contact with the outside world and considered my options. Angling at The Sanctuary was top of my list. A perfect venue for my escape, it was remote, isolated, quiet, and undisturbed, presenting the ideal antidote to the bone-aching stresses of work.

Four hours later, I was lying in long grass next to the soothing waters of The Sanctuary, my bait cast out and with my eyes closed as I allowed the silent mountain to coax me into a partial sleep. This was the true value of The Sanctuary, to allow things to exist outside the ever-maddening world. The carp, which had been living there for hundreds of years, were oblivious to city high-rises, work-related stress and microwave popcorn. They had their own world and were probably awaiting the return of the monks from over the hill. Today, they had just me: a lone angler intent on nothing more than slowing down the pace of his day; to relax, regain his sanity and reflect upon the importance of wild carp in today's world.

It had taken many years of searching to discover The

WILD CARP

FREEDOM AND FORGIVENESS

Sanctuary. My journey had started as a schoolboy, when the world appeared innocent and time seemed to last forever. The world and my circumstances had changed, yet the image of the wild carp and the purpose of angling had remained constant. The simple joys and childlike excitement of seeing a float dipping as a fish grabbed the bait, the adrenaline of viewing a large fish appearing from the deeps; both are primeval instincts that modern technology is unable to steal. By feeling these emotions, we remain alive and independently human. It's a far cry from a busy modern life where we are corralled into a pre-defined existence: a mould that determines our daily routine, the badge we wear, and the age when we are deemed to be beyond usefulness. The thought of work, while lazing at The Sanctuary, would appear like a lightning bolt to the brain.

The speed of modern life is an oppressive thing. The corporate world is quick to punish those with an honest heart. Qualities such as 'nice, honest, kind, happy, relaxed, sincere, innocent' are frowned upon as weaknesses. Yet these values are the essence of a good person and are the building blocks of one who would seek the purity of angling. Unfortunately, if you don't keep the balance, they can be lost like sand through your fingers. That's why angling for wildies is more important now than ever before. The notion of fishing for ancient strains of carp is, in itself, an adventure into the past, where we rediscover joys that connect us to emotions experienced by our ancestors. It's a subliminal portal to a previous age, evoking memories of youth, when life was slower, simpler and much more fun. Thus it's a great excuse for good, honest, escapism and fantasy. If we choose to dress like Toad of Toad Hall when fishing for wildies, or stop everything for afternoon tea and cake, then so be it. 'Twee' gets my vote. As Jerome K. Jerome said, "Once we discover how to appreciate the timeless values in our daily experiences, we can enjoy the best things in life." However, he also said, "I can see the humorous side of things and enjoy the fun when it comes; but look where I will, there seems to me always more sadness than joy in life." Thus there's also a serious side to our subject when considering the wild carp's need for conservation. The innocence and fragility of the true wild carp of the Danube epitomises, like so many other endangered species, how human progress has disadvantaged or destroyed the natural world. Once there was a time when all carp were wild, at first in the great seas of the Middle East and then in the mighty River Danube. They were then captured and tamed by man, distributed across the globe and 'mutated' into the bloated creatures we know today. 10,000 years of natural evolution skewed in two millennia. We are responsible for our actions. But we must battle for sufficient time in our own lives to bring value to our existence and give back to the natural world from where we came. These ancient carp of The Sanctuary, for example, exist

WILD CARP

FREEDOM AND FORGIVENESS

because they are isolated. The entire strain could be destroyed overnight with the introduction of modern carp breeds, or carp viruses, or pollution, or predation. We are obliged to ensure that old strains of carp are preserved. We seek not for forgiveness but – like these carp – the freedom, space and time to exist.

I remember Nicholas whom I met at The Monastery Pond. This peaceful man was happy to exist humbly and for the moment. There was no mention of the future, or if he planned to leave the protection of the monastery, or get a job, or immerse himself back into the business world. I learnt something from this. We are so blinkered by progress, so preoccupied with where we want to go and how fast we can travel, that many of us have lost the ability to simply 'stop'. Angling for wild carp forces us to press the pause button. It is a slow and contemplative art, where we can lie back and do nothing for hours, or days, or weeks, while waiting for a bite. There are few activities in life where we are not criticised, let alone rewarded, for such a lazy 'abuse' of time. Yet this apparent inactivity is the whole point of the act. Angling allows us to defocus our minds. It enables the waters or the motionless float to hypnotise us into a state of contentment. Dreaming of wild carp, or fishing for wild carp, enables us to drift on the tide of contentment towards a golden shore. And when we are there, we may imagine ourselves gazing upon that which sustains us: an image of angling unlike any other. Of ancient golden carp, lost in time, that glide beneath the surface of the known to coax us into the natural undercurrents of life. They are meditation for the mind and food for the soul.

2009

XXV

THE MIST OF BELIEVING

Some will say that searching for your dreams is like looking for unicorns in an emerald forest. And when searching for wild carp they'll say that neither the fish, nor the place, exists. They will say that following a golden thread will lead only to a king, dethroned and living in the gutter. This may be so. But the king was made, not born. The crown was never his to wear.

The path of those who search for wild carp is not laid out in black and white, like a zebra crossing upon a busy road. It is a web of adventures that leads to a central point, a conclusion that highlights the importance of the quest: that they are searching for something that can only be discovered by those who *believe*.

Lost treasures? Or fool's gold and chartered seas? Only by searching will you find out. My advice is to dive deep and make your discovery. But doing so will require you to hold your breath for a very long time. Be patient, persistent and above all, believe.

My friend Phinehas accompanied me on many wild carp adventures. He had a way of keeping us going when we discovered yet another pond full of tarnished king's gold, or felt we were getting short of air. He'd walk us to the top of the nearest hill, where we'd sit and stare at the horizon. Then he'd say, "My Friend, if ever the adventure proves tiring, or you lose sight of your dream, look to the west at sunset. There, on days when the skies are clear, you might see upon the horizon a thin layer of golden mist. When it appears, you will know its purpose: it is the mist of believing."

The mist doesn't show itself to everyone; you have to want to see it. You have to believe. It's this believing – in hidden waters and long-lost strains of ancient carp – that sustains the quest.

What did my quest prove? That these fish, these dreams, are there. Somewhere. Waiting to be discovered.

BONUS CHAPTERS ABOUT WILD CARP

Bonus Chapter

XXVI

RETURN TO THE FOLLY

Do you remember the story of Keiya – the great carp of the Folly that billowed into the mist of legend? She represents the fish that was always in my dreams, always uncatchable, during the twenty-year journey of this book.

Alas, Keiya is no more and our quest for wildies is complete. Or is it? Keiya remains in my dreams, as mist that shrouds my earliest memories and fogs my attempts to retrace my footsteps. She ushers me forward, towards other lakes and yet more undiscovered families of wild carp. She reminds me that there's always something over the horizon: undiscovered lands and adventures waiting to happen. But they are the quests of tomorrow. Wouldn't it be nice to go back in time, just this once, to relive a past adventure? To experience and savour things as they happen; to be there, seeing, hearing, smelling, and feeling everything first-hand. No words written in the past tense; instead, real time observations that act as a portal through time. Well, we can do just that. Such is the power of a journal. So I turn to the mud-encrusted pages of my favourite diary, the one that lived in my fishing creel during 2009. There, from February of that year, is the story I've read more than any other. Of a day when I fished at BB's Folly. Let's relive that special day as we read the Journal in its original form.

The Folly Pool, mid-Wales, Friday 27th February

I'm writing this while sitting beside my favourite pool, a lake known as The Folly. It's a water that exists somewhere between my imagination and the sanctity of the Welsh mountains, a place of hope where I live out my dreams. It's a secret place, known only to a privileged few. Finding it involves more than a map, because the meniscus between the real world and the dream world, where the pool is to be found, presents itself as a mirror to both realms. To see more than a reflection requires us to filter what we see, to view the world with honest eyes. Only then is The Folly revealed.

The Folly is a dark pool of great depth, surrounded by oak and beech trees, some of them several hundred years old; their boughs spread far out across the lake, in some places intertwining, creating a cavernous feel that shields the pool from its surroundings. I'm relaxing beneath one of these trees right now, gazing out across the surface of the water towards my ivory-tipped float. I know it to be a swan quill whipped in burgundy silk, but right now it could be a pink flamingo's feather dancing the foxtrot. I'd hardly take notice. I'm preoccupied –

and most content – with the nature around me, while I sit here penning my thoughts. I'm going to write about whatever happens, or comes to mind, as it happens, so that you can experience events 'live'. I want you to sense that you are here with me, at this special place, sharing the adventure.

You and I have not been here long (it is mid-afternoon) as I opted to get a few jobs done before leaving home. The day started sunny and warm, so my optimism was high as I loaded the car with my fishing and cooking equipment. But alas, as is often the way when travelling west, the skies grew cloudier and the air cooler as I drove the hundred-odd miles to the Black Mountains.

As I turned off the main road, and headed down a narrow lane, I could see snow on distant mountaintops. It shone brightly, even beneath grey skies, such was the clarity of the winter air. I wound down the car window so that I could breathe it all in. The air smelled pure and fresh. So crisply cold, yet invigorating and life giving. I craved to be outside the car, savouring the peacefulness of the silent moors. But I drove on, conscious of my lateness, and aware that I was meeting a friend at the pool.

My first glimpse of the pool, as seen through bare branches of lakeside trees, was of dark peaty water surrounded by a ghostly halo of lichen-crusted branches. It was an ethereal, wintry scene, contrasted by the signs of spring at my feet, where celandines and snowdrops were flowering and daffodils were pushing up from the ground. They were defiant, like me, to the frosts of winter. For whoever thought of fishing for wild carp in the middle of winter? It's hardly the classic image of balmy summer evenings. But then, in winter, one's fishing can be interrupted by more cups of tea, especially when there's a warm and welcoming cottage in which to drink. It opens up a whole new meaning to the term 'pleasure fishing'. (If, indeed, we do any fishing at all.)

Predictably, my friend Angelus was sipping a cup of tea when I arrived at the cottage. The teapot was still warm, so I poured a cup of Priory finest while we sat talking and drinking. We chatted for two hours; such is the pleasure of reliving stories of seasons past.

2pm came. Angelus and I decided it was time to go fishing. We shouldered our creels, picked up our rods and nets, and walked down to the lake. Angelus pointed to a spot adjacent to the far bank where he'd pre-baited with maggots; this would be where he'd fish. I fancied the nearside margin of the lake, as the overhanging branches and deep water made me hopeful of intercepting a patrolling fish. (This all sounds very technical, but the reality is that our swims were opposite each other, a mere thirty yards apart. Our plan was to do some social fishing, where we could see each other and call to each other without shouting.)

BB centrepins ready for some wildie fishing

Angelus and I walked to our respective swims, tackled up, and cast our lines into the pool. We soon saw signs of fish. A shoal of wildies was mooching in and around a fallen tree to my right and Angelus' left. Each fish was dark and moderately well concealed in the water. They appeared as shadows, until one would rise and flick its dorsal fin up through the surface of the water, or bow wave, or roll and flash its golden-yellow belly.

Two sprinklings of maggots from Angelus' catapult had the carp nosing and grubbing around the bottom of the lake for their afternoon meal. Before long, the lake's surface was speckled with clusters and streams of bubbles from feeding fish.

That was an hour ago. The fish are still there, infuriatingly so. They insist upon eating all our free baits while refusing to get caught. Angelus and I keep missing bites. We're both using quill floats fished lift method (where only a single shot is placed on the line, which rests on the bottom, cocking the float at the correct depth; if a fish picks up the bait, it lifts the shot and the float rises). Our floats are lifting, and wiggling, and flopping over. They might as well be sticking two fingers up at us, because no matter what they do, we don't seem to be able to hook a fish. At first we thought all this activity was from scamps (small carp from last year's spawning), but then we'd miss a bite and see a substantial bow wave shoot off across the lake.

The number of bites we're missing has become ridiculous. We're getting two bites per minute, all of which result in a float flying over our shoulder and a defamatory remark echoing across the lake. Actually, it's becoming quite funny. Angelus and I are playing a sort of 'cursing ping pong' as each of us misses a bite. He'll miss a bite, swear, and then I'll do the same.

Nothing silly, just a growing hilarity as we realise how hopelessly bad we are at catching fish. (Ah. Perfect timing. I've just heard the 'swish' of Angelus' rod and then a shout of "Damn it!" followed by an urgent request for a fork and some rowlocks.) Actually, I think Angelus is getting more bites than me, as I've had time to write these words. So I guess that makes me the duffer of the party.

I'm now sitting away from the lake's edge. The fish have moved closer to the bank and I've slowly drawn my float back towards them. It sits in the water, cocked at about sixty degrees (the most aesthetically-pleasing angle for a float, in my opinion), about fifteen feet from the bank. It hasn't moved for a while. But I don't mind. It sits perfectly in its surroundings.

All is calm, which puts me at absolute ease. I can't find exactly the right description to describe how I feel. I could use the word 'ahh', but it doesn't quite work. Instead, I'll just exhale deeply and feel my shoulders relax. I'll roll my head from side to side. I'll close my eyes and lie back onto my wax jacket, which is draped across the ground behind me. I'll keep my eyes closed and listen to the soft rasping noise of air being inhaled slowly through my nostrils. My chest will enlarge to its capacity, and then I'll exhale, releasing all the tension from my body until I find myself drifting away with the fishes.

It might be February, but spring is in the air.

It's certainly warm enough to sleep outdoors on an afternoon like this. I can hear the calls of robins, blue tits, blackbirds, rooks and a buzzard. If I opened my eyes I could probably see a tree creeper scurrying up a tree trunk overhead. And there! A squirrel might be jumping from tree to tree, climbing to the end of the beech branches to eat the plump leaf buds. Amongst the branches twines a honeysuckle in full leaf. Oh how I look forward to summer evenings, when the perfume from that plant will fill the air. Time to unwind, to savour the sweet bliss of inactivity.

Wait a minute. Oooh! I say again: "Oooh!" My float twitched just then. I am startled, switching quickly from naturalist's observations to hunter's instinct. My hand draws close to the handle of my rod. There! Again! A dip! It's going to go! It's going, it's go-

Damn it! Another missed bite. At least I have an opportunity to change the maggots on the hook and cast again. Actually, what's that commotion?

Yes! Angelus is into a fish! He's finally hooked one. This is it!

Correction. Angelus has just lost a fish. (Cue even worse swearword from Angelus and a noise that sounded like someone blowing down a rubber didgeridoo.)

I do hope we get a fish. Conditions are perfect.

At last! Angelus is connected to a fish, good and proper. He's standing up to play it, so it must be putting up a fight. It's certainly making a splashy kafuffle under his rod tip, but oh my, Angelus' bamboo rod is bending into an almost impossible arc. C'mon Angelus. Catch us a fish!

Yes! Yes! The fish is in the net! Angelus has done it! A winter wildie, from The Folly, on the most perfect of days.

Stay here and watch my float while I go round to see the fish.

Angelus' wildie from the Folly

Okay. I'm back. The carp was a scale-perfect wildie weighing 9lb. (It's unusual for us to weigh a fish, but this winter capture meant that we just had to record its weight.) The fish's colours were brilliant: deep chestnut brown (almost black) on the back and shoulders, blending into a deep bronze and then brass on the flanks, with a golden-copper belly. It looked as old as the lake – a black carp of the Black Mountains.

How did Angelus hook that fish when we'd missed all other bites? He said that he had to let the fish run with the bait until he saw the line slithering across the surface of the water. Only then did he strike. It's got to be worth a go, so I'll try it when I next get a bite.

I've just recast. A gentle underarm swing was enough to get the bait and float into position: just to the right of an overhanging bramble and far enough from the snag to enable me to stop a fish. And now, a sprinkle of maggots around the float. That's it. I'm okay to settle back down on my jacket and await my next bite.

There. We're back fishing.

Five minutes have passed. No bites as yet, but the fish are still here, and feeding. I can see clusters of bubbles appearing on the surface, caused by the fish disturbing the silt around my hookbait.

Hang on. That's interesting. The float has just wobbled. It's-

Woomph!

Wow. That was amazing. The bite. The fight. The

fish. I repeat: "The fish!" We have another wildie on the bank (well, in the landing net, anyway). Angelus is on his way here with the camera. While we wait for him to get here, let me tell you about the capture.

The bite was perfect. The float lifted about an inch, wobbled from side to side, and then flopped over before sliding away in the direction of the snag, pulling line across the surface behind it. I followed Angelus' advice and waited a few seconds before I grabbed the rod and struck into the fish. I felt its weight, but that was all. It was as if I'd hooked an underwater branch. The fish did nothing! It just remained motionless in mid-water, not knowing that it was hooked. I gradually increased the pressure on the fish, drawing it up in the water and slowly towards me.

And then it woke up.

The lake erupted with bow waves scattering everywhere. One of them was followed by my line, which zipped through the water, creating a sound like fabric being torn in two. I clamped down hard on the reel. The water boiled as the fish turned. It lunged against the rod, and then plunged deeper in the water, sending up a cloud of silt and bubbles. And then the water 'lifted' in one almighty boil. The fish was on the bottom, in eight feet of water, and yet had displaced the surface of the pool with the power from its tail. The sight took me aback. The boil was a good ten feet across. *Just what had I hooked?*

Hopeful, even in winter

RETURN TO THE FOLLY

The Folly is reputed to contain large wildies; fish approaching twenty pounds were witnessed in the 1970s but none have since been seen. The fish on the end of my line was so powerful. I'd caught wildies to twelve pounds from here before, but this was stronger. It fought harder. And more determinedly. And yet, judging by its delayed response when I hooked it, I wonder whether it had been frozen solid or simply didn't know what was going on?

With the fight drawing closer to the bank, I was able to control the fish's runs. It tired and I was able to lift it in the water. It rolled on the surface and I was able to see it for the first time. It had the telltale dullness to its scales that told me it was a very old fish. It was perhaps the most ancient-looking wild carp I'd ever seen, and with a tail fin that waved at me like two hands placed side by side.

Holding the fish on a tight line beneath the rod tip, I was able to prevent it from getting its head down and picking up any more speed. It wallowed on the surface, allowing me to scoop it from underneath with my landing net.

The fish was mine. On a day when everything was perfect, I'd caught the ultimate wild carp.

Aha! Angelus is here. Time to fetch the carp from the landing net in the margins and photograph it for prosperity.

There. All done. Photographed and returned.

But not weighed. To do so would ruin the dream and destroy the legend of such a phenomenal carp. For this was a fish that will bless or haunt our dreams, getting bigger each time we relive the tale until such time as we believe, or remember, that it might just have been Keiya who graced us with her presence. Proudly defying the naysayers, the monarch of the pool might not be dead after all...

When years of searching culminate in an hour's blissful activity, one realises that wild carp really are the pinnacle of everything one hopes for as a traditional angler. In fact, right now, I believe that angling doesn't get any better than this. I'm glad that I was able to share it with you. Perhaps, when we think about everything that's gone before, we'll relive the adventure all over again, or go in search of new waters and new hopes for the discovery and future of this most special type of fish.

To the humble, unassuming, timeless and infinitely mysterious wild carp: we thank you for our adventures, and for proving that dreams really can become real.

BONUS CHAPTER

XXVII

THE WILD CARP OF THE DANUBE

Priory Slovakian correspondent Pavol 'Pali' Timko fishes the River Danube – the natural home of the true wild carp – and has caught these genuine fish. Following the publication of the magazine version of this book back in 2012, Pali contacted me to discuss his experiences. Here's a transcript of that very special conversation.

Fennel: In the UK, the wild carp is the Holy Grail of the traditional angler. How is the fish perceived in Slovakia?

Pali: Wild carp are called "sazan" in our country. Per definition they are the original wild subspecies that survived thousands of years in the Danube and its tributaries. Though domesticated carp have been bred for about two millennia, sazan seem to spawn in different areas and that is the answer to why they still exist. This species is considered critically endangered due to vanishing spawning habitats. Though carp in general is eaten in our country, sazan is protected by law. It wouldn't be possible for an angler to specialize in sazan because in our legal system it would be unacceptable to target a protected fish; nevertheless sazan are sometimes caught accidentally, which was my case.

The water that you fish – the river Danube – is Europe's second-longest river and very different to the traditional ponds of Britain. Could you describe the river where you fish, telling us about the features, wildlife and characteristics?

When the Danube leaves the Alps it reaches the Pannonia basin, also called the inland delta. The distributary system is like a maze with jungle-like forests. To the southwest is Hungary, northeast is Slovakia. Along the white line border there is the old Danube but the majority of water flows through the artificial new channel (banned for anglers) that feeds the biggest hydro plant in Slovakia. The biggest challenge with this type of water is to locate fish because the water surface is huge. Carp are nomadic and the water here is full of fallen trees, which makes good for escaping fish. From time to time we face floods but the dam decreased this danger. Nature is incredible here, with birds, animals – beaver returned recently. Just beware – mosquitos make hell out of this environment in summer.

The Danube must pose a daunting challenge to the angler.

My main interest has focused on distributaries, streams that branch off and flow away from the main river.

The key to success is finding the right spot. Wild carp like hideouts, the vicinity of streams and oxygenated water but close to groups of fallen trees is the key. You may see many trees around and yet find no carp in the vicinity. It seems to me that combination of rocky riverbed and trees is important. Also the food sources must be around. Clusters of mussels may make your fishing hard (their sharp shells can cut line) but they are natural food for carp. Swims like this can be approached only from a boat. Too far from the trees and you will have no takes. Too close and fish may be become tethered if you don't know how to play them safely away from the snags. The secret is to find a very dense underwater snag. I've found that carp may escape towards such a snag but will not enter into it, especially if the fish is not bothered by the strong pull of an angler.

Is it possible to specifically target wild carp?

No. It is illegal to target sazan in my country. And don't forget, scientific research says you have less than 0.1% chance to land a wild sazan carp. I read a scientific article from the 1980s that told of an ichthyology survey where 6,276 carp caught from the Danube contained only 18 sazans and only 3 of them were original wild carp without slightest doubt. To catch such a fish is like winning the lottery. Consider this: I caught one sazan in 1998, two in 2006 and one in 2009.

WILD CARP

The question that's really burning is 'what is it actually like to hook and play a true wild carp?'

They are tireless fighters. That is the key characteristic. One of my fish was 87cm long, weighed 9 kilo (around 20lb) and its capture is a memory that will never be forgotten. From my peg, I placed my bait onto a rocky slope behind a sunken dam. The top of the sunken dam is 1.6m deep and the slope goes down to an 8m hole, fallen trees are very close. When I placed the bait I saw this carp jump like a dolphin out of the water and I was speechless for a while. I thought, "Oh my God, such a fish, I would love to have it on my line!" And yes, the take came later. I looked at the tip of my rod and it was shivering. So I hit the rod. I felt the fish on the other end and jumped into the boat. The fish swam into long weeds so I had to rip off the plants by hand, only then could I pull the carp out and yes, it was still there and with a little luck I was successful. When I pulled it out to the free water, the carp went mental and my boat turned three times by 360 degrees as the carp pulled me along like Moby Dick. The fight took for sure longer than thirty minutes and it required fine work handling the electric motor with one hand and the rod with the other. Even when landed, the carp continued to fight on my unhooking mat that was placed so close to the water that the fish managed to jump back into the river. I was lucky because there were dense weeds and I jumped into

THE WILD CARP OF THE DANUBE

Pali with his big Danube wild carp

Note the lack of notch or lump from head to shoulders

the water to retrieve the escaping carp. My wife, who took the photo, laughed so much that she was almost unable hold the camera.

You mentioned the knocking on your rod tip when the fish took the bait. Is this typical?

In all instances sazan took the bait and didn't run; they simply stayed there. I believe that mussels are the natural food to sazan. My concept is that they pick up mussels that are many times connected by sort of threads and by shaking their head they try to break off this fibre. Mussels are extremely sharp so I believe carp misevaluate a hook as a mussel stuck in their mouth. This shivering was visible on the rod tip. I struck and a carp was there. So this is definitely a specific sign very different to all the other Danube carp I've caught.

A true wild carp in the net. Wow! Can you describe how you felt when you first caught one?

In 1998 I didn't know much about wild carp beside the fact they are protected and must be released after capture. Also at that time I was not much involved in carp fishing. But in 2006 I knew I'd achieved something extraordinary and I was in a state of positive shock. The feeling was supported after a meeting with ichthyology professor K. Hensel who was amazed when I showed

THE WILD CARP OF THE DANUBE

A muscular wild carp from the Danube

him my photos and he stated that he believed that sazan is more or less extinct. He studied photos and said that they are sazan carp without any doubt. He showed me the bones of a sazan carp found in an archaeological survey from a settlement near the Danube, dated, if I remember right, 2500 B.C.

Could you describe how the true Danube wild carp looks and how it differs from the king carp in the river?

There is a lack of pronounced hump behind the head. The body is lean (at least 1/4 ratio) and its profile is more round and very muscular. The fins are stronger in general and rather greyish. The mouth is turned a bit more down than with domesticated carp.

Do you know of any historic stories about wild carp in your stretch of the Danube or in neighbouring regions?

Honestly, not really. Sazan carp is almost like Yeti or Big Foot. Some speak about it but almost nobody could see it with their own eyes. The Danube is really a treasure and wild carp seems to be the jewel in the crown.

Finally, I heard that there's a 'secret' pond in Slovakia where the true wild carp is preserved. Could you describe it to us?

It's not a secret pond; it is a small reservoir in the village of Velčice. Fishing is prohibited. There is a non-profit organization that brought this lake into existence in cooperation with a state run ichthyology institution. It was stocked with genetically checked 100% sazan carp.

It's reassuring to know that the Sazan's future is safe in a protected environment. Pali, thank you. What you've shared with us is inspirational.

Bonus Chapter

XXVIII

THE WILD CARP OF WALES

As an all-round traditional angler, I fish 'seasonally' for a variety of species at different waters and at different times of year. Because of this, I have often faced the dilemma of having too many favourite fishes. There are so many beautiful species to angle for, each with their unique charm, that it's not easy to select the best. Both vie for the top spot depending upon the time of year that I'm asked to choose. (Trout always win in spring, wild carp in summer, barbel in autumn and grayling in winter.)

Significantly, both wild trout and wild carp are pure versions of species 'corrupted' by fish farmers. Each has brash and unsightly relations that they don't mention in polite conversation, and each represent a wild (or feral) creature in a wild environment. Hence, the angler may connect with a little piece of angling heaven.

For me, the nirvana for both species exists in the rugged and isolated mountains of Wales.

It was 1988 when I first became interested in wild carp. Mr Hackney, my physics teacher at school, was an angler and learned of my love of fishing. He lent me two books: *Confessions of a Carp Fisher* by 'BB', and *Casting at the Sun* by Chris Yates. They were pure gold, a revelation. Homework obligations were ignored, friends abandoned. I read both books within a week. The result? A mission: to find overgrown and forgotten ponds and lakes inhabited by ancient strains of 'wild' carp.

Looking back, and in re-reading those two books, I'm surprised that I didn't immediately spot the authors' references to the best waters. I was so preoccupied with the sense of adventure that I didn't see the obvious clues to specific wild carp lakes and areas. It took me twenty years to discover that the very best pools – subtly referenced in *Casting at the Sun* – are to be found in and around the Black Mountains of Wales. Here the landscape is rugged, with craggy windswept llyns (the Welsh name for mountain lakes) and peaks that hint at the explosiveness of pre-history.

Some of the oldest strains of carp live in 'forgotten' Welsh llyns. Strains of fish rumoured to have been stocked by the Cistercian monks in the 11th century. The combination of ancient lineage and outstanding scenery makes fishing for wild carp in Wales seem like an act of reverence. Nowhere have I savoured such a sense of enlightenment while angling. A man can find God in such places.

I usually begin the traditional coarse fishing season on 16th June by fishing at a wild carp lake called the

Folly. Not so this year. My desire for solitude was too great. I needed to water my roots and connect with a piece of living history. Instead, I would return to the Welsh mountains where I first became an angler, and fish for the wild carp of mid-Wales.

Pant-y-llyn (which I call 'The Sanctuary') is my favourite wildie lake. It sits 1,400 feet up a mountain, so the views across the Welsh counties are spectacular. Free from the pressures of modern angling, it encourages a simple approach and an honest heart. Never a place for boilies or bolt rigs, or (I hope) a carbon rod, it's somewhere I've visited in the past and been content not to cast a line – such is its appeal to the poet in me. Instead I have laid back and relaxed in the grass beside the pool, looking up at the sky and watching buzzards and red kites circling overhead. Fishing there is a personal experience, an act of leaving one's troubles behind and rediscovering the boyhood pleasures of angling. And I'm grateful that my articles about wild carp have encouraged others to fish there as well, to savour things first hand. This chapter is about celebrating their fishing, while pursuing an adventure there myself.

Writing about one's favourite lakes is a delicate task, ensuring the most private pools are protected while more public ones are revealed. Photographs enable so much to be shared – especially when comparing one's catches. So here's a mini photo album, shared before I begin my return to The Sanctuary.

Andy Roberts with his first Welsh wildie

A fly-caught wildie from Llyngwyn

Stu Harris with possibly the best example of a Welsh wildie

Scott Winstanley braving the cold at Pant-y-llyn

Andy Batchelor with a wildie from Pant-y-llyn

Nigel Evans with a Welsh wildie

THE WILD CARP OF WALES

Les Darlington enjoying a 'mild summer' at Pant-y-llyn

Peter Whipp with a Llyngwyn wildie

The first gather of wild carp enthusiasts, August 2014

Waiting for the reel to spin at Pant-y-llyn

THE WILD CARP OF WALES

Fennel and Stu Harris with a Llyngwyn wildie

The Sanctuary, 16th June 2010

I arrived at Pant-y-llyn at 2pm – a late start considering the season began at midnight. Normally I would have been fishing at dawn, but I'd decided upon a leisurely start and a cooked breakfast before travelling to the lake. By the time I arrived, the afternoon sun had warmed the air to a swelter and there was an absence of wind to cool my brow – or ripple the surface of the pool. The wildies were active when I arrived: rocking and swaying the dense beds of weed that fill the lake for all but a small circle in its centre. Every now and then a golden-scaled fish would leap into the air and land with a crash that shattered the calm.

However, the wildies were not active in the lake's shallow margins as usual. Instead, they were moving sixty to seventy yards out in the centre of the pool. This proved challenging, given that I'd only brought an 8ft stalking rod, centrepin reel, a packet of hooks and a large loaf of bread with me. With no weights or 'controller' float, I'd be unable to cast further than a 'freelined' range of twenty feet.

I catapulted small pieces of breadcrust towards the carp, steadily reducing the range of the free offerings in an attempt to draw the fish closer to me. As expected, the carp found and ate the pieces of bread that were furthest from me. But they wouldn't come any closer.

I looked again at the water, noticing that its level was

twelve inches lower than usual. Perhaps the water in the margins was too shallow for the fish to safely explore in daylight and the weed was too dense to grant them access to their usual feeding zones? My only option (other than standing back and observing the fish) was to strip off and wade out into the lake, where I might get to within casting distance of the fish.

I removed all my clothes and immediately felt the sun burning my back and buttocks. Being fair skinned, I would only be able to tolerate the rays for a few minutes else I'd develop an unwanted shade of 'cooked lobster'. So, being a sensible angler, I half-filled my flat cap with slices of bread and placed it on my head. I then strode into the water with the dignity of knowing that I wasn't *totally* naked.

I waded purposefully yet slowly through the weed-beds, feeling the hornwort brush across my legs and nether regions. With my arms held above my head, I carried my rod like a soldier holding aloft his gun as he crossed a swamp. I stopped fifty yards from the bank, The water now was chest high and lapping my armpits. Horseflies, intent on drinking my blood, were attacking my shoulders and neck and I was beginning to wonder whether this was a good idea after all. My eyes, however, were locked on a wildie rising twenty feet in front of me.

I continued to inch forward until I was within ten feet of the fish. With the weed being so thick, the fish

WILD CARP

Discretely 'tackle out', but with a respectable-looking wildie

On top of the world at Pant-y-llyn

was oblivious of my presence.

I lowered my rod, removed a chunk of bread from beneath my hat, and attached it to the hook on my line. Then, in a 'ducks in a barrel' act, I lowered the bait onto the carp's snout. The fish took the bait instantly.

I struck and, amidst an explosion of spray, hauled the fish towards me across the weed and to my hand. I held the carp tight to my body, turned around, and then waded back to shore.

I threw on a shirt to save me from burning, then photographed the carp, observing how sleek it looked compared to its chunkier cousins, then returned it to the lake. The fish, my first of the season, weighed perhaps two pounds.

My season had begun with a day of blue skies, brilliant sunshine, near-naked wading and wildies. It was classic start to the traditional coarse fishing season.

I craved nothing more from life, and I certainly didn't yearn to cast again. I knew, in the depth of my heart, that the adventure was complete.

Bonus Chapter

XXIX

WILD CARP IDENTIFICATION

The wild (Sazan) carp is now a critically endangered species in its native River Danube. Cultivated 'King' carp are the ones found in most waters. Fortunately for the wild carp enthusiast, cultivated carp regress towards a wild-like shape with each generation spawned in the wild. These feral fish are known to anglers as 'wildies'. The goal is to discover a very old strain of carp – possibly several hundred years old – that have almost completely reverted to a wild shape. This guide will help you identify these very special fish.

Three types of carp are shown:
- the first is a king carp, which the wildie enthusiast should avoid. If they are present in a water, then the strain may be ruined if they have cross-bred with the original (older strain) of fish. Mirror and leather carp (those with few or large scales) and fully scaled common carp fit into this category.
- second is a wild carp
- third is a feral carp, which is a king carp strain that is reverting back to its wild-type form.

Domesticated/cultivated King Carp
(also known as a Common Carp)

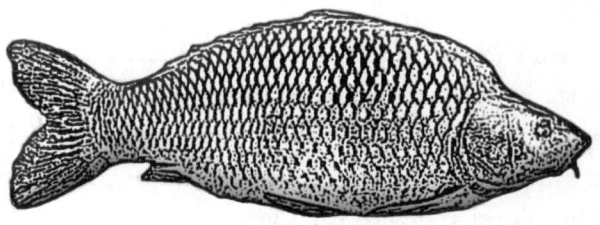

- Notch or hump where the head meets the shoulders (the more cultivated the strain, the larger the hump)
- Deep and broad body, with a pronounced belly
- Large mouth with long barbules (sometimes over three inches long)
- Rounded, lobed tail with a thick 'wrist' where it meets the body
- Can grow to over 50lbs
- The carp shown here is an example of a European fish-farm strain, bred to grow quickly and put on weight. It appears more rounded than many classic 'English' king carp.

Wild Carp Identification

Wild Carp
(example shown from the Danube)

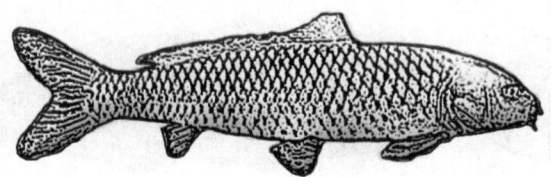

- No notch or hump where the head meets the shoulders (feral forms have a slight notch)
- Long, streamlined, torpedo-shaped body, tapering towards the tail
- Often has a very blunt 'snout' to the head
- Small mouth with relatively short barbules
- Pointed, noticeably-forked tail
- Fns often appear large for the size of fish, and have a noticeable dark grey-brown colour.
- Scales of older strains may be a dull brassy-bronze colour rather than golden
- Rarely grows to more than 10lbs

Feral Carp
(also known as wildies or wild-type carp)

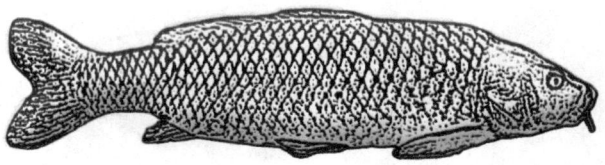

- Small notch where head joins the shoulders
- Long, streamlined body
- Rounded, lobed tail, with a broad wrist where it meets the body
- Can grow to 20lbs or more
- The older the strain (number of generations of reversion from king carp to feral carp), the more wild-like the feral fish will appear.
- The fish shown here is a relatively young strain of feral carp. It still has the shoulders and deepish belly of a common carp, and the wrist of the tail is broad.

Bonus Chapter

XXX

FURTHER READING

Origin and Domestication of the Wild Carp
Eugene Balon (1995)
The definitive research paper on wild carp by the world's leading authority. Covers the origin, evolution and distribution of carp across the world; good focus on the Danube wild carp, Roman links and medieval cultivation.

The Early History of the Carp and its Economic Significance in England
Christopher Currie (1991)
Research paper highlighting the introductions and growth in popularity of carp in Britain. Good information about the reasons why carp were introduced to the lakes surrounding country houses. Theories around carp imports between 1100 and 1400 are speculative.

WILD CARP

FURTHER READING

Carp strains held at the Fish Culture Research Institute, Svarvas, Hungary
Bakos and Gorda (2001)
Details the different carp strains held at the living gene bank in Hungary. Includes photographic references. Of interest to wild carp enthusiasts are the Hungaran Tisza wild carp that spread westwards to Europe and the Russian Amur wild carp that spread eastwards to Asia.

Diversity of Common Carp Genetic Resources
Kohlmann, Gross and Murakaeva (2005)
Scientific research paper looking at wild and domesticated strains of carp in Europe and Asia. The research highlights the fragility of the wild carp gene pool due to hybridisation and the removal of natural habitat.

A History of Carp Fishing Revisited
Kevin Clifford (2012)
Well-researched book on the history of carp fishing in the UK. The first chapter discusses wild carp and the introductions of cultivated carp to the UK. Famous waters, anglers and catches are also featured. A glimpse into a cherished past.

Stu Harris, Matt Tanner and Fennel Hudson in 2013, celebrating a very good idea about the preservation of wildies.

Bonus Chapter

XXXI

WILD CARP CONSERVATION

I'd like to end this book with an idea: one so powerful as to make us realise that we're only just at the beginning. The idea stems from a conversation between Stuart Harris, Matthew Tanner and myself on the banks of Llyngwyn in 2013, where we discussed the vulnerability of the oldest strains of carp and our obligation to protect them. Why? Because there are perhaps fewer than a dozen waters containing early medieval strains of carp in the UK. The fish are so at risk from predation, pollution, cross-breeding with king carp, or simply that their owners don't understand their value, that they need our help. How wonderful and responsible it would be for us to create an organisation dedicated to the conservation and appreciation of wildies? Perhaps it would be a charitable trust, or a not-for-profit community interest group, committed to educating people about these historic fish and, through funds raised, establishing a breeding programme and securing waters where wildies could be given safe homes? What do you think? Maybe, by the time you read this, it might be more than an idea…

www.wildcarptrust.org

ABOUT THE AUTHOR

FENNEL HUDSON

"Author, artist, naturalist and countryman. His is a lifestyle to inspire the most bricked-up townie."

Fennel Hudson is a traditional angler who seeks the timeless atmosphere of overgrown and forgotten pools. He caught his first wild-like carp at the age of 15. This inspired him to dedicate twenty years to the pursuit of medieval strains of carp. The quest led him to discovering some of the UK's oldest bloodlines and brought him into contact with other wild carp enthusiasts such as Chris Yates and Mike Winter. Together they found a world of imagination and adventure, with wild carp at its centre. This gave Fennel a unique perspective of the true beauty (and humour) of life, which he shares by reminding us to 'Stop – Unplug – Escape – Enjoy'.

For more information please visit:
www.fennelspriory.com

THE FENNEL'S JOURNAL SERIES

Fennel's Journal

Issue 1 · Christmas 2011

The Meaning of Life

THE FIRST-EVER REVIEWS OF FENNEL'S JOURNAL:

"Fennel's Journal began as a series of illustrated letters to friends. As these evolved they became less a diary, more a manifesto, and the Journal is now exactly that – a way of living, rurally and simply: very real for all those who recognise the importance of tradition and joy."

Caught by the River

"I can see where it might lead. What he has would make amazing TV. It's the Good Life, but in a realistic way. It's Jack Hargreaves. It's Countryfile. It's quality Sunday newspaper stuff. It's 1948, all over again. In trying to escape the present he's inevitably created a brand. A potentially very powerful brand."

Bob Roberts Online

"Fennel's Journal is a masterpiece about rural living. It is a route-map to the life we all seek."

The Traditional Fisherman's Forum

From A Meaningful Life:

"Life is the most beautiful and rewarding gift. We just need to take time out to allow us to reflect, change perspective, and see things in their best light. Sometimes we just have to stop and feel the pulse of the Earth, the rhythm of the seasons and the internal voice that was once our childhood friend. As the natural world grows smaller, so too does its intensity and the size of the window through which it may be viewed."

NO.1

A MEANINGFUL LIFE

A Meaningful Life is the first and perhaps most important Journal. It documents the origins of Fennel's Priory and why Fennel decided to live by a new set of ideals. With themes ranging from escapism, adventure, work-life balance, identity and purpose, through to traditionalism and country living, it sets the scene for future editions – building messages that are central to Fennel's Priory. Ultimately it conveys the importance of a relaxed, balanced, and meaningful life.

READER TESTIMONIALS

"I loved reading this Journal. It's inspiring and has the beginnings of something very special."

"Fennel's chosen trajectory is firmly in the slow lane. He's a countryman, with courage to stand behind his traditional values."

"Witty and emotive, Fennel's writing conveys passion for a slower-paced and quieter life."

From A Waterside Year:

"Water is intrinsically linked to the mystery and excitement of discovering new worlds. Of dreams. And hopes. And thoughts of what 'could be'. Dreams free us from normality. ...As the daydreams grew longer, the distinction between what was real and what was imaginary grew less. Soon I existed in a blissful world of my own creation. Reality, as I learned, is only a matter of perception...A life that is real to one is surreal to another."

NO. 2

A WATERSIDE YEAR

In *A Waterside Year*, Fennel takes time out to live beside a lake in rural England. Here he appreciates the healing qualities of water, studies the wildlife around him, lives at the pace of someone outside of normal daily life, and discovers the freedom that's found in isolation. Getting so close to Nature, and spending time in idle fashion, enables him to discover a stronger sense of self. Ultimately he learns that freedom is not a place, but something that exists within us.

READER TESTIMONIALS

"A year in the wild. How we would all love to follow in Fennel's stead and indulge our dreams, to come out the other side a stronger and wiser person."

"A Journal with a message – that we should take time out to think about what's important, and see the beauty of the world."

"A truly blissful read full of inspiration and humour. The story of Fennel sitting in his tent, with the noises outside, had me laughing out loud!"

From A Writer's Year:

"Writing, with a fountain pen and ink from a bottle, is the simplest of things. Yet it can transport us to a different place entirely. Imagination is the real magic that exists in this world. Look inwards, to see outwards. And capture it in writing."

NO. 3

A WRITER'S YEAR

A Writer's Year celebrates the writer's craft. It champions the handwritten letter, discusses vintage pens and writing ink, and celebrates things such as antique typewriters and the quirkiness of the creative mind. It's a blend of observations. It's funny. It's serious. It's real life. But most of all it is written to encourage aspiring authors to find their voice, to put pen to paper, and follow their dreams.

READER TESTIMONIALS

"Worth it for the first chapter alone. It cannot fail to motivate and inspire the would-be author."

"What Fennel has written is not so much a eulogy for the handwritten letter as a call-to-arms for everyone to follow their dreams and make the most of their God-given talents. This is a genuinely inspiring read."

"I loved the part: 'If a pen can communicate our thoughts, dreams and emotions and be the voice of our soul, then ink is the medium that carries the message'. It shows how important and generous writing can be."

From Wild Carp:

"Some will say that searching for your dreams is like looking for unicorns in an emerald forest. They will say that following a golden thread will lead only to a king, dethroned and living in the gutter. This may be so.
But the king was made, not born.
The crown was never his to wear.
...If ever the adventure proves tiring, or you lose sight of your dream, look to the west at sunset. There, on days when the skies are clear, you might see upon the horizon a thin layer of golden mist. When it appears, you will know its purpose: it is the mist of believing."

NO. 4

WILD CARP

Angling for wild carp is about adventure, history, atmosphere and emotion. *Wild Carp* captures this aplenty, describing Fennel's 20-year quest to find a very special type of fish. But it's also about nature connection and a desire to uncover the seemingly impossible – a place where we can discover and live out our dreams, to completely indulge the mantra of 'Stop – Unplug – Escape – Enjoy'.

READER TESTIMONIALS

"When written well, traditional angling writing by the likes of BB, for example, is the type of literature that I can read again and again. Fennel's writing flows un-hurried without overly romanticising each point and the research is thorough; from the first sentence I was thinking, 'this lad can write!' It's informative and very refreshing."

"Such inspiring writing. His words 'Somewhere in the undergrowth of the impossible' had me staring out from the page in amazement. Fennel's writing is pure poetry."

From Fly Fishing:

"The deeper we travel into the natural world, and the greater the number of technological encumbrances we leave behind, the more likely we are to escape the fast-paced lifestyle and stresses of the 21st Century.
For some, angling enables a quest into the unknown, an adventure into the wild. For these fortunate folk, fly-fishing is escapism. Their hours by water serve as contemplation to enrich their souls, directing their quest inwards, towards their longed-for state of completeness."

NO. 5

FLY FISHING

Fly Fishing celebrates the most graceful and artful form of angling, explaining what it means to be an angler – in the spirit of Izaak Walton – and how fly fishers differ from bait fishers. The sporting and aesthetic beauty of fly-fishing is described in Fennel's usual witty and contemplative style. As he says, "Fly fishing is the ultimate form of angling; it gives us a reason to fish simply, travel lightly, and explore wild places that replenish our soul. With a fly rod, we're not casting to a fish; rather to a circle of dreams: ripples that spread into every aspect of our lives".

READER TESTIMONIALS

"Brilliant writing. Fennel made me laugh out loud in bed. My wife was asking questions!"

"A delightful, well-articulated, read. I strongly recommend it, especially to the contemplative, tradition-loving, bamboo fly rod devotees among us."

"A very inspiring and rewarding read. I will try to tie the Sedgetastic fly. It looks tasty!"

From Traditional Angling:

"Physics teaches us that for every action, there is an equal and opposite reaction: a natural balance of energy that sustains the equilibrium of life. In modern angling, these forces are skewed so far in favour of technology that the balance between science and art has been lost. But there is a movement, an undercurrent that defies the flow of progress. There are those who choose not to follow the crowd. They seek not to fish in a predictable, scientific manner. They yearn for the opposite, to buck the trend, *to be different*. They are the Traditional Anglers."

NO. 6

TRADITIONAL ANGLING

Traditional Angling celebrates the Waltonian values of angling: about fishing in a seasonal and uncompetitive way for the pure pleasure of being beside water. It wears its heart on its sleeve and a wildflower in its lapel. It's passionate, provocative and eccentric, written for those who appreciate the aesthetics of angling and uphold its sporting traditions. So, with great enthusiasm, raise your bamboo rod aloft for an adventure that proves there's more to fishing than catching fish.

READER TESTIMONIALS

"A beautifully written, very engaging and hugely enjoyable read. In fact, it's the best thing on fishing I've read in a long time."

"What a Journal! Fennel is clearly the spiritual successor to his mentor – the great Bernard Venables. There's so much wisdom and craftsmanship in his writing. Bernard clearly taught him very well."

From The Quiet Fields:

"The countryside, with its vast horizons, fresh air and ever-changing seasons is, by its very nature, more life-giving and adventurous than any amount of modern indoor living. It inspires a love of natural history – everything from the birds that sing in the trees to the quality and richness of the soil beneath our feet. Most of all, it creates the desire to exist more naturally. And in doing so, we appreciate the balance of life."

NO. 7

THE QUIET FIELDS

The Quiet Fields is rooted in the humus-rich soil of the countryside. It's about remote rural places where Nature exists undisturbed, where we may sit and ponder 'The Wonder of the World'. The Journal tips its hat to these places, and to the nature writing of BB, revealing the 'Lost England' that still exists if you know where and how to look. It is the most sentimental and astutely observed Journal to date, discussing the 'true beauty' of Nature. If you've ever yearned to hear birdsong during a busy day, then this is the book for you.

READER TESTIMONIALS

"Fennel's writing reminds me of the works of Roger Deakin. It inspires me with faith in the quiet life and that although I may be isolated, I am certainly not alone."

"Fennel has captured the essence of the countryside – that is, its almost human character. So brilliantly has he compared and contrasted it with the nature of we humans. It's not so much a 'balanced study', more a 'study of the balance' between Nature and Man."

From Fine Things:

"It seems that, depending upon which side of the thesaurus-writer's gaze we sit, one's uniqueness as a person can be deemed to be either eccentric or distinctive. Both, in my opinion, are good...As we get older, and experience more things, those of us with strength of character and a sense of purpose will grow stronger and fight harder; those who lack identity and direction might end up sitting in a corner somewhere, blindly taking all the knocks that life throws at them. What does this teach us? That character and purpose are directly linked to confidence and conviction. What links them? Courage – to be oneself, no matter what others might say."

NO. 8

FINE THINGS

Fine Things celebrates the special and sentimental items and activities that convey our personality. The writing is fast-paced, quirky and humorous, reflecting the author's enthusiasm and eccentric view of the world. But be warned: if you look inside Fennel's mind, you might see a hula-hooping hamster named Gerald, shaking his maracas, loudly banging a bongo, and getting him into all sorts of trouble. So strap yourself in. This book picks up pace and takes some unexpected turns. From the deeply personal to the outright eccentric, it's for those who seek to be different.

READER TESTIMONIALS

"A very fine thing, indeed. Fennel's best and funniest book to date. He is the only author who can make me laugh out loud and cry in the same sentence. I was constantly in tears, for all the right reasons."

"Deep in places, outright bonkers in others. A demonstration of the fine line between genius and madness."

From A Gardener's Year:

"Roll up your sleeves and imagine your vision of paradise. This, in whatever form it takes, is your garden. Keep hold of the image; know it's every detail and piece together the elements that need creating or nurturing, so that when you get the chance, you can prepare the ground, sow the seeds, and make it real. Ours is a gardener's life, whether we realise it or not."

NO. 9

A GARDENER'S YEAR

A Gardener's Year celebrates the joy of growing things and reflects upon a life working with plants. But it's not a record of horticultural activities through the seasons. It's a metaphor for having a dream and making it come true. For Fennel, who has spent half his life working in gardens, it's about cultivating a cottage garden where he can aspire to a self-sufficient lifestyle. The Journal sees him sow the seeds of this future reality.

READER TESTIMONIALS

"Fennel's writing is uniquely funny. I mean, who else can name a chapter 'Chicken Poo'? His sense of humour, balanced with some deep yet subtle messages, had me in tears. From his 'escape' to a public toilet, to what not to say to a celebrity, this is a Journal to entertain all readers."

"When I started reading this Journal I had a garden with a lawn and a patio. Now I have a vegetable patch, blisters, an aching back, and the biggest smile of my life. Thank you Fennel!"

From The Lighter Side:

"If self-actualisation is the pinnacle of one's development, then it can't be achieved if your mountain has two peaks...Being the 'best version' of yourself implies that you have other versions kept locked in a closet. Don't have any 'versions'. Just have one true, beautiful and pure form of you.
So climb your mountain, open your arms to the Creator who greets you there, and sing loudly to the world that stretches out beneath you.
Write your name permanently on the landscape of your mind.
Remember: you are a child of Nature. And you are free."

NO. 10

THE LIGHTER SIDE

There's a delicate balance between something meaning a great deal and that same thing becoming so serious that it's ludicrous. (Ever got stressed about what clothes to wear for an interview?) That's why *The Lighter Side* provides the encouragement, humour, anecdotes, reflections and honesty that are essential to Fennel's message of 'Stop – Unplug – Escape – Enjoy'. After all, we can only 'Enjoy' if we know how to smile when we get there.

READER TESTIMONIALS

"The Lighter Side was more than I expected. The deeper meaning within it – and the devastating honesty it conveys – made me question exactly where I am in my own life and what I can do to improve it for my family and me in the time that remains. Thank you Fennel for opening my eyes and adjusting my course."

"The opening chapter is the most startling, erudite, compassionate and open piece of writing I have ever read...thank you Fennel for sharing so much. It did and does mean a great deal."

From Friendship:

"What I'm talking about is proper friendship. The sort that is authentic, genuine and real. Where we can look into the eyes of another person and know what they're thinking. ...Because, as friends, we remember 'why' as much as 'when' or 'what'. Through good times and bad, we were there. Together. That's the bond, the unquestionable obligation that's freely given. It's the tightest hug, the biggest kiss, the tearful hello and the widest smile. If that's what it means to be a friend, or an extrovert, or just someone who cares for others then that's me to the last beat of my heart."

NO. 11

FRIENDSHIP

Written by the Friends of the Priory, with bonus chapters from Fennel, *Friendship* provides insights into what it means to be friends, how shared interests and beliefs support collective purpose, and how, when we're together, we can achieve more, appreciate more, and have more fun. It's about the broader world of Fennel's Priory and how it exists in others. It's a book written 'for us by us', with friendship as the theme.

READER TESTIMONIALS

"Possibly the greatest gift that this Journal bestows is to let us know that we are not alone."

"Like friendship itself, this Journal brings together people and meaning. It reminds us that 'together we are strong'. Thank you Fennel for leading our charge."

"The message (and evolution) of Fennel's Journal is most evident in this Friendship edition. With such obvious themes as identity and legacy, it's clear that what Fennel has shared over the years is a route-map to freedom and a stronger sense of self."

From Nature Escape:

"I am once again seeking an escape, to where I hope to find freedom and connect with the young man who handed me his trust ten years ago. This will be a faithful interpretation of the Priory, a fitting way to mark ten years of writing. As I said at the end of last year's Journal, 'One's journey through life is not linear; it's circular.' So let's go back to the beginning, and rediscover the quiet world."

NO. 12

NATURE ESCAPE

Nature Escape provides the most detailed account of a day that follows the motto of 'Stop – Unplug – Escape – Enjoy'. In it Fennel returns to the woodland of his youth to study its wildlife and savour its peacefulness.

Written in real-time, with twenty-four chapters that each represent an hour, the Journal is an account of how time spent outdoors in wild places enables us to observe the nature that's around us *and* within us.

READER TESTIMONIALS

"Fennel's Journal has always provided us with an escape, but now we know where the escape can lead. As promised, it leads to enjoyment – and very enjoyable it is too!"

"24 hours alone in a wood, with only 'the wild' for company? With Fennel as our guide, there's no such thing as 'alone'; only the warmth of knowing that quiet times are the fine times."

"By studying the nature within us and around us, Fennel demonstrates how to be 'at one' with nature."

From Book of Secrets:

"There's a greater man than me who can sum up our journey, a mountaineer who in 1865 first climbed the Matterhorn. Edward Whymper, over to you: 'There have been joys too great to be described in words, and there have been griefs upon which I have not dared to dwell, and with these in mind I say, climb if you will, but remember that courage and strength are naught without prudence, and that a momentary negligence may destroy the happiness of a lifetime. Do nothing in haste, look well to each step, and from the beginning think what may be the end.'"

NO. 13

BOOK OF SECRETS

Book of Secrets links all editions of Fennel's Journal together. With 14 Journals in the series, and 14 core chapters in this book, it's the 'one book to bind them all' with each chapter providing the continuity story from one Journal to the next.

Containing Fennel's previously private writing, it provides deep insight into the Fennel's Journal story. If you've ever wondered why each Journal is themed the way it is, or tried to find the metaphor in each edition, then *Book of Secrets* is for you.

READER TESTIMONIALS

"What a privilege: being able to read the private writing of my favourite author. Book of Secrets is a treat."

"Such honesty and wit. Fennel puts into words what I have only ever thought, or dare not say."

"Fennel's Journal really is a series – it's meant to be read as a whole. And now we have the key to unlock it."

From The Pursuit of Life:

"We can hide, or we can strive – for a life of our making. With endless possibilities and opportunities to reach for our dreams, we owe it to ourselves to dream big and keep going, irrespective of what we might encounter. Sadly, the thing that most limits our success is not others, but ourselves. How strongly we believe, how confidently we act, how fiercely we react, how passionately we want, and how life-affirmingly compelled we are to grow and blossom; that's how we keep going, no matter what, to be the person we want to be, living the life we deserve, in dreams that are real."

NO. 14

THE PURSUIT OF LIFE

The Pursuit of Life concludes the Fennel's Journal story. It's a reflective tome that provides Fennel's commentary on the journey and a 'behind the scenes' view of the challenges and rewards of a life rebuilt on one's terms.

It's an account of how the series came to be and how it evolved, and includes much of Fennel's private writing, several of the original handwritten drafts, correspondence between The Friends, and encouragement for those on similar paths. Ultimately it shows how the Fennel's Journal series can be used as a route map to a more fulfilling life.

READER TESTIMONIALS

"A life retold, for our benefit. Fennel is to be congratulated for everything he's achieved – on paper and in life."

"It's his life in the books, but it could so very easily be ours. Fennel has a way of seeing truth in the severe and the sublime, and bringing it home."

"Can this really be the end? When dreams are real, we never wake from them. More books Fennel, please!"